Surviving the Nuclear Winter

Andrew Parry

Published by Andrew Parry, 2024.

While every precaution has been taken in the preparation of this book, the publisher assumes no responsibility for errors or omissions, or for damages resulting from the use of the information contained herein.

SURVIVING THE NUCLEAR WINTER

First edition. December 10, 2024.

Copyright © 2024 Andrew Parry.

ISBN: 979-8230125037

Written by Andrew Parry.

Table of Contents

Introduction: Living in a Post-Nuclear World 1

The Day After: Facing a New Reality 2

Understanding Nuclear Fallout and Its Effects 4

Radiation Poisoning: Symptoms and Survival 6

The Nuclear Winter: Preparing for a World without Sunlight 8

Building a Safe Haven: Shelters and Protective Measures 10

Identifying Hot Zones: Where to Avoid and Why 12

The Science of Radioactive Particles: What You Need to Know 14

Staying Clean: Decontamination Techniques for People and Pets 16

Testing the Air: Tools and Methods for Measuring Radiation 18

Water Safety: Purification and Storage after Fallout 21

Food Contamination: Identifying and Avoiding Tainted Supplies 24

Growing a New Eden: Safe Gardening in a Contaminated World 27

Livestock in the Fallout: Raising Animals for Safe Consumption 30

The Invisible Enemy: How Radioactive Particles Spread 33

Protecting Your Family from Radiation Exposure 36

Radiation and Health: Long-term Effects and Coping Strategies 39

Medical Preparedness: Treating Radiation Wounds and Poisoning 42

Surviving the Cold: Strategies for the Nuclear Winter 46

Mental Health in the Apocalypse: Coping with Trauma 49

Understanding Radiation Levels: The Tools to Measure Exposure 52

Fallout Myths and Facts: Separating Truth from Fiction 55

Radioactive Soil: Challenges and Solutions for Safe Cultivation 58

Protecting the Vulnerable: Caring for Children and the Elderly 61

Waterborne Radiation: Risks in Rivers, Lakes, and Oceans 65

DIY Radiation Shields: Crafting Your Own Protective Gear 69

Adapting Diets for Safety and Survival 73

The Science of Mutation: What Radiation Does to Life 76

The Importance of Hygiene in a Contaminated World 80

Creating a Fallout-Proof Wardrobe: Clothing for Safety 83

Long-Term Shelter: Reinforcing and Upgrading Your Safe Haven 87

Understanding Radiation Decay: How Time Changes the Danger 90

Protecting Your Eyes and Skin: Combatting UV and Radiation Damage 93

How to Recognize and Avoid Secondary Threats 97

Clean Meat: Raising Radiation-Free Animals 101

Radioactive Zones: Maps and Indicators for Survival 105

The New Weather Patterns: Living with Post-War Climate Change 109

Managing Limited Resources: Making Every Drop and Bite Count 112

Renewable Energy for Survival: Harnessing Post-War Resources 116

Adapting to a Hostile Environment: Living with Radiation 120

The Role of Technology in Survival: Tools You Can Use 124

Making Do with Less: Survival Skills for Limited Resources 128

Emergency Communication: Staying Connected When It Matters Most 131

Bartering and Trade: The New Economy in a Broken World 135

Community Survival: Working Together in the Aftermath 139

Clean Energy in the New World: Finding Safe Power Sources 143

Scavenging Safely: Finding Supplies Without Risk 147

Preparing for the Unpredictable: Adapting to Changing Conditions 151

Alternative Medicines and Remedies for Radiation Sickness 155

Rebuilding from Rubble: Starting Over After Destruction 159

Community Survival: Working Together in the Aftermath 162

Navigating the Ruins: Travel Safety in the Post-Nuclear World 166

Bartering and Trade: The New Economy in a Broken World 170

Fire Safety in Fallout Zones: Managing Risks in Destruction 174

Protecting the Next Generation: Teaching Children Survival Skills 178

Preserving Knowledge: Libraries and Education in Survival 182

Post-War Government: Navigating New Power Structures 186

Introduction: Living in a Post-Nuclear World

Imagine a world transformed overnight by unthinkable devastation—a world where the familiar has been replaced by rubble, and the comforting predictability of modern life has given way to uncertainty and survival. In the aftermath of a nuclear war, humanity faces a stark reality: survival is no longer a given; it is a battle fought each day, requiring ingenuity, resilience, and a profound understanding of the new world we inhabit.

This book is a guide to navigating that harsh reality. It is written with the assumption that nuclear war has already reshaped the globe, leaving us to confront its consequences head-on. The fallout is more than just radioactive particles; it is the crumbling of societal structures, the fragility of ecosystems, and the profound psychological toll on survivors. Yet, amidst the devastation lies the undeniable will to endure, rebuild, and adapt.

We will explore the challenges of this post-nuclear world: how to protect yourself and your loved ones from radiation poisoning, how to navigate the dangers of nuclear winter, and how to measure and assess the invisible threats in the air, water, and food around you. We will discuss the essential practices for growing clean food, keeping livestock safe, and creating shelters that protect against radioactive fallout. Just as importantly, we will delve into the human element—how to care for children, foster community, and preserve knowledge to ensure that survival extends beyond mere existence.

This book also recognizes the enormity of the task ahead. Surviving in a post-nuclear world is not just about techniques and tools; it is about mindset and determination. It is about transforming fear into action, despair into purpose, and chaos into opportunity. Each chapter offers insights and practical steps to help you not only live but thrive in this transformed world.

Though the topic is daunting, the tone of this guide is conversational and empowering. It is meant to be your companion, offering clarity and guidance in a time when uncertainty reigns. Whether you are a lone survivor or part of a community, this book aims to equip you with the knowledge and confidence needed to face the challenges ahead.

The road to survival will not be easy, but it is possible. Together, we can navigate this new reality, preserve what is essential, and work toward a future where humanity not only endures but finds a way to flourish once more. Welcome to the first steps of living in a post-nuclear world.

The Day After: Facing a New Reality

The day after a nuclear war is a moment of grim reckoning. The world as we knew it has changed irreparably, and survival now becomes the only priority. As dawn breaks, you find yourself peering into a landscape shrouded in uncertainty. The sun, if visible at all, is dimmed by the thick layers of smoke and debris thrown into the atmosphere. Streets are eerily silent, broken only by the occasional distant sound of collapse or the muffled cries of others trying to comprehend the devastation. In this chapter, we will explore what the immediate aftermath looks like and how to navigate it, both physically and mentally.

The first realization is the absence of reliable infrastructure. Power grids are down, communication networks are silent, and water supplies are either disrupted or contaminated. The structures you once depended on for food, healthcare, and safety have been obliterated or rendered inaccessible. In this void, confusion reigns, but survival depends on swift and clear-headed action.

The most immediate danger is radioactive fallout. This invisible, deadly threat consists of fine particles of radioactive material thrown into the atmosphere by nuclear explosions. These particles gradually settle back to the ground, contaminating everything they touch. Fallout is most dangerous during the first 48 hours after a detonation, as its radioactivity is at its peak. Seeking shelter during this period is crucial. If you are already in a basement or an enclosed space, stay there. The thicker the walls and the further you are from the outside, the better your protection.

If you are caught outside, your priority is to find cover. Avoid touching surfaces or items that might be contaminated. Once you find shelter, remove your outer clothing carefully to avoid spreading radioactive dust and wash exposed skin with soap and water. Remember, the goal is to minimize exposure as much as possible in these critical early hours.

The psychological impact of such an event cannot be overstated. Fear, panic, and grief are natural responses, but these emotions, if unchecked, can paralyze you at a time when action is necessary. Ground yourself in the reality of your situation. Focus on what you can control—securing food, water, and a safe space. Acknowledge your emotions, but don't let them dictate your actions. Survival is a mindset, and staying calm can save your life.

Food and water, the two essentials for human survival, become immediate concerns. However, these resources are likely to be contaminated with radioactive particles. Do not consume water from open sources like rivers or lakes unless it has been tested and purified. The same applies to any food exposed to fallout. If you had the foresight to stockpile non-perishable food and bottled water, these will be invaluable now. If not, scavenging must be approached with extreme caution. Sealed cans and packages are generally safe, but thoroughly wash them before opening.

Communication is another critical challenge. Radios, particularly battery-powered or hand-crank models, may be your only link to the outside world. Emergency broadcasts can provide vital information about safe zones, evacuation routes, or government aid, if such systems are still operational. However, you must also prepare for the possibility that information may be sparse or unreliable. Trust your instincts and prioritize your immediate needs.

As hours turn into days, the reality of nuclear winter begins to set in. The thick clouds of soot and ash in the atmosphere block sunlight, plunging temperatures and disrupting weather patterns. The reduced sunlight affects plant growth, further complicating food production. This is not just a cold, dark season—it is an ongoing battle for survival against a hostile environment.

Beyond the immediate physical needs, community becomes a lifeline. If you encounter others who are also seeking to survive, banding together can provide mutual support and shared resources. However, be cautious. Desperation can drive people to unpredictable behaviors. Trust must be earned, not assumed.

The day after a nuclear exchange is the starting point for a long, arduous journey. The landscape may be unrecognizable, but humanity has survived devastating catastrophes before. Knowledge, preparation, and resilience are your greatest allies as you navigate this new reality. In the face of overwhelming destruction, remember that every small step towards safety and stability is a victory. The world has changed, but survival means adapting to that change, one moment at a time.

Understanding Nuclear Fallout and Its Effects

Nuclear fallout is one of the most misunderstood and terrifying consequences of a nuclear exchange. Its invisible nature makes it especially dangerous, as you cannot see or smell the particles that can cause harm. Fallout consists of radioactive materials that are blasted into the atmosphere during a nuclear explosion. These materials settle back to the ground over time, contaminating everything they touch—air, water, soil, buildings, animals, and people. To survive in a post-nuclear world, it's essential to understand what fallout is, how it behaves, and the specific dangers it poses.

When a nuclear bomb detonates, it generates a massive fireball that vaporizes everything in its immediate vicinity. This vaporized material mixes with radioactive elements from the bomb itself, forming a dense plume of smoke and ash that rises high into the atmosphere. This is the iconic mushroom cloud often associated with nuclear explosions. As the plume cools, the radioactive particles it carries begin to fall back to Earth. The closer you are to the detonation site, the sooner fallout will begin to settle and the more intense its concentration will be.

Fallout is most dangerous in the first 48 hours after a detonation. During this time, the radiation levels from the particles are at their highest. These particles emit gamma rays, beta particles, and alpha particles, each with varying degrees of penetration and harm. Gamma rays are the most dangerous because they can pass through the body, damaging internal organs and tissues. Beta particles are less penetrating but can still cause severe skin burns and damage if inhaled or ingested. Alpha particles are the least penetrating but are deadly if they enter the body, as they can directly damage cells and tissues.

Understanding the concept of radioactive decay is vital when dealing with fallout. Radiation levels decrease over time as the radioactive isotopes lose their energy, but the rate of decay varies by isotope. For example, iodine-131, a common by-product of nuclear explosions, has a half-life of about eight days, meaning its radiation intensity halves every eight days. Cesium-137, another fallout component, has a much longer half-life of about 30 years, making its effects more persistent. This is why some areas may remain uninhabitable for decades or even centuries.

The effects of fallout exposure depend on several factors, including proximity to the blast, duration of exposure, and the type of shielding available. Acute radiation sickness is a common consequence of high-level exposure and manifests in symptoms like nausea, vomiting, diarrhea, and severe fatigue within hours or days. Long-term effects include an increased risk of cancer, genetic damage, and organ failure. Even low-level exposure over an extended period can lead to chronic health problems.

Fallout does not spread uniformly. Wind patterns, weather conditions, and the geography of the area determine its dispersion. A nuclear explosion in a windy region can carry fallout hundreds or even thousands of miles away from the detonation site. Rain can exacerbate fallout by washing radioactive particles from the air onto the ground, creating "hot spots" of high radiation. Understanding the local weather and wind patterns can help you predict fallout distribution and avoid the most dangerous areas.

Protection from fallout involves minimizing exposure, decontaminating surfaces, and avoiding ingestion or inhalation of radioactive particles. Staying indoors, preferably in a well-sealed and shielded space like a basement or inner room, offers the best immediate protection. The more dense and thick the materials surrounding you—such as concrete, lead, or packed earth—the better your shielding from gamma rays.

If you must go outside after fallout has begun to settle, limit your time and wear protective clothing. Cover as much skin as possible, and use a respirator or improvised mask to avoid inhaling particles. Once you return indoors, remove your outer clothing carefully to prevent spreading contamination and wash exposed skin with soap and water.

Food and water safety is another critical concern in fallout zones. Open water sources like lakes, rivers, and reservoirs are likely to be contaminated, as fallout particles settle on their surfaces or wash into them. Water from sealed underground wells or stored in sealed containers is much safer. Food, especially fresh produce and livestock, can absorb radiation directly or become contaminated by fallout settling on it. Consuming sealed, pre-packaged food and water is the safest option until contamination levels decrease.

In addition to immediate survival concerns, understanding the psychological effects of living in a fallout-contaminated environment is important. The stress of constant vigilance, limited resources, and fear of radiation can take a heavy toll on mental health. Knowledge about fallout and its behavior can help mitigate some of this stress, as you'll be better equipped to make informed decisions for your safety.

Finally, tools like Geiger counters or dosimeters are invaluable in assessing radiation levels in your environment, water, and food. Learning how to use these devices before an emergency occurs can save your life. Monitoring radiation levels regularly allows you to make informed choices about where to go, what to eat or drink, and how to avoid prolonged exposure.

Nuclear fallout is a formidable enemy, but it's not an insurmountable one. By understanding its nature and effects, you can take steps to protect yourself and your loved ones. Knowledge, preparation, and vigilance are your strongest defenses in a world transformed by nuclear catastrophe.

Radiation Poisoning: Symptoms and Survival

Radiation poisoning, also known as acute radiation syndrome (ARS), is one of the most immediate and life-threatening effects of exposure to high levels of radiation. In a post-nuclear world, understanding the symptoms, treatment options, and survival strategies is essential for safeguarding yourself and those around you. Radiation poisoning occurs when radioactive particles penetrate the body, damaging or destroying cells at a level that disrupts normal biological functions. The effects can range from mild to fatal, depending on the dose and duration of exposure.

Radiation exposure is measured in units called sieverts (Sv) or rems, and the severity of radiation poisoning correlates with the dose received. A dose of 1 Sv may cause mild symptoms, while exposure to 4 Sv or more can result in severe sickness and a high likelihood of death without prompt medical intervention. At doses exceeding 8 Sv, survival becomes almost impossible due to catastrophic damage to internal organs and tissues.

The symptoms of radiation poisoning manifest in stages, and the progression depends on the level of exposure. The first stage, known as the prodromal phase, occurs within hours to days after exposure. Symptoms include nausea, vomiting, diarrhea, headache, and fatigue. These symptoms are your body's immediate response to cellular damage and are often mistaken for other illnesses. If you or someone else begins exhibiting these symptoms after a nuclear event, it's crucial to assume radiation exposure has occurred.

Following the prodromal phase, there may be a latency period during which symptoms temporarily subside. This deceptive calm can last from hours to weeks, depending on the radiation dose. Unfortunately, the absence of symptoms doesn't mean the danger has passed. During this time, damage is continuing at a cellular level, especially to rapidly dividing cells such as those in the bone marrow, gastrointestinal tract, and hair follicles.

As the body's systems begin to fail, the third phase, or manifest illness phase, sets in. Symptoms during this phase are severe and vary based on the primary systems affected. For those with bone marrow syndrome, the destruction of white blood cells leads to a weakened immune system, leaving the body vulnerable to infections. Gastrointestinal syndrome results in severe diarrhea, dehydration, and electrolyte imbalances. At higher doses, cardiovascular and central nervous system syndrome occurs, characterized by confusion, loss of consciousness, and rapid death due to brain swelling or heart failure.

The key to surviving radiation poisoning is minimizing further exposure and managing symptoms effectively. The first step is to distance yourself from the source of radiation. If you suspect exposure, seek shelter immediately in a building with thick walls or underground spaces, which can reduce radiation levels significantly. Once sheltered, remove contaminated clothing and place it in a sealed bag or container to prevent further spread of radioactive particles. Wash your body thoroughly with soap and water, paying close attention to exposed areas like the face, hands, and hair.

Medical treatment for radiation poisoning focuses on addressing symptoms and preventing complications. If professional medical help is unavailable, first aid measures can still make a difference. For example, rehydration with clean water or oral rehydration solutions is critical for combating dehydration caused by vomiting and diarrhea. Managing infections is also a priority; if antibiotics are available, they can be lifesaving for those with weakened immune systems. If burns or wounds are present, cleaning and covering them with sterile dressings can prevent infection and promote healing.

In cases where high doses of radiation have been absorbed, substances called radioprotectors or chelating agents may help reduce the body's radioactive burden. Potassium iodide (KI), for instance, can protect the thyroid gland from absorbing radioactive iodine, a common fallout contaminant. However, KI is only effective if taken shortly before or immediately after exposure. It does not protect against other types of radiation or provide immunity to radiation poisoning.

Nutrition also plays a significant role in recovery. A diet rich in antioxidants, vitamins, and minerals can help the body repair damage and boost the immune system. Foods high in vitamin C, E, selenium, and zinc are particularly beneficial for counteracting oxidative stress caused by radiation exposure. However, ensure that food and water are free from contamination before consumption.

Psychological resilience is another crucial factor in surviving radiation poisoning. The mental toll of dealing with the illness, coupled with the broader challenges of a post-nuclear world, can be overwhelming. Maintaining a positive outlook, focusing on actionable steps, and seeking support from others can help mitigate the psychological impact.

Long-term effects of radiation exposure include an increased risk of cancers, particularly leukemia and thyroid cancer, as well as potential genetic damage that can affect future generations. Regular monitoring for symptoms and medical checkups, if available, can help detect and manage these risks over time.

Radiation poisoning is a daunting challenge, but survival is possible with prompt action, knowledge, and preparation. By recognizing the symptoms early and taking appropriate steps to limit exposure and treat the effects, you can increase your chances of surviving and even thriving in a world altered by nuclear catastrophe. In the face of such adversity, understanding and adapting to the realities of radiation poisoning is both a necessity and an act of courage.

The Nuclear Winter: Preparing for a World without Sunlight

The term "nuclear winter" describes the catastrophic environmental consequences of a large-scale nuclear war, where massive amounts of soot and ash are propelled into the atmosphere, blocking sunlight and drastically altering the Earth's climate. This phenomenon plunges the planet into a prolonged period of darkness and cold, with devastating effects on agriculture, ecosystems, and human survival. Preparing for nuclear winter requires not only a deep understanding of its consequences but also practical strategies to endure and adapt to this harsh new reality.

When nuclear explosions occur, the resulting firestorms consume vast swaths of cities and forests, sending enormous quantities of particulate matter into the upper atmosphere. These particles form a dense layer of soot that reflects sunlight back into space, reducing surface temperatures worldwide. This sudden and dramatic cooling disrupts weather patterns, creating a cascade of effects that include shorter growing seasons, crop failures, and widespread famine. The impact is not localized to the war zones; it becomes a global crisis.

The first step in preparing for nuclear winter is understanding its immediate and long-term implications. Without adequate sunlight, photosynthesis slows or stops, affecting plant growth and the entire food chain. Temperatures can plummet by several degrees, creating conditions similar to an ice age in some regions. Rainfall patterns shift unpredictably, leading to droughts in some areas and flooding in others. These environmental changes compound the challenges of survival by making traditional agriculture nearly impossible.

Food security is one of the most pressing concerns in nuclear winter. Traditional farming will not be viable in the absence of sunlight and normal weather conditions. Preparing for this involves stockpiling long-lasting, non-perishable foods like canned goods, freeze-dried meals, and grains. These supplies should be stored in cool, dry, and secure locations to ensure their longevity. Additionally, learning alternative food production methods, such as hydroponics or growing nutrient-dense microgreens indoors under artificial light, can provide a sustainable food source in the absence of outdoor agriculture.

Water security is equally critical. With disrupted weather patterns, clean and accessible water sources may become scarce or contaminated. Having a robust water purification system, whether through filtration, boiling, or chemical treatment, is essential. Collecting rainwater or accessing underground water sources can also help ensure a steady supply of potable water.

Shelter during nuclear winter must not only protect against radiation but also provide insulation against the extreme cold. Underground shelters or well-insulated buildings are ideal, as they can maintain a more stable temperature. Sealing windows and doors with plastic sheeting and duct tape can prevent drafts and minimize heat loss. If fuel sources like wood or propane are available, stockpiling them for heating and cooking will be invaluable. However, these resources must be used judiciously to ensure they last through the prolonged period of nuclear winter.

Energy independence becomes a vital aspect of survival. With sunlight scarce, solar panels may become less effective, making alternative energy sources like wind turbines, hand-crank generators, or even bicycle-powered generators more reliable. Having access to a backup power supply can mean the difference between enduring the cold and succumbing to it.

Psychological preparedness is just as important as physical readiness. The darkness and cold of nuclear winter, combined with the isolation and stress of survival, can take a severe toll on mental health. Finding ways to maintain a sense of purpose, routine, and connection with others is critical. Activities like journaling, crafting, or storytelling can provide a sense of normalcy and help pass the time. If you are in a group, fostering a spirit of cooperation and mutual support can strengthen everyone's resilience.

Nutrition becomes a delicate balancing act during nuclear winter. With limited access to fresh produce and meat, deficiencies in essential vitamins and minerals can arise. Stockpiling vitamin supplements and learning to grow high-nutrient crops like sprouts and algae indoors can help mitigate this. Protein sources such as canned beans, nuts, or preserved meats should also be prioritized to maintain energy and strength.

Another critical challenge is preserving health and hygiene in an environment where resources are limited. Basic medical supplies, including first aid kits, over-the-counter medications, and wound care items, should be part of any preparation plan. Preventing the spread of illness in close quarters requires strict attention to cleanliness and waste management.

Community networks, if they exist, can be a lifeline during nuclear winter. Sharing resources, skills, and knowledge can improve everyone's chances of survival. However, trust and communication are essential to avoid conflict and ensure fair distribution. If venturing out becomes necessary, having a plan for safe travel and protection against the cold and radiation is crucial.

Finally, it's important to think long-term. Nuclear winter may last for months or even years, but it will eventually give way to a new equilibrium. Preparing for this eventuality involves storing seeds for hardy crops, learning skills like permaculture and foraging, and acquiring tools for rebuilding infrastructure. Adapting to a changed environment will be a slow process, but human ingenuity and resilience have overcome dire circumstances before.

Nuclear winter is one of the most harrowing scenarios humanity could face, but preparation and adaptability can make survival possible. By understanding the challenges and taking proactive steps to address them, individuals and communities can endure even the darkest and coldest of times. In the absence of sunlight, hope and determination can still provide the warmth needed to carry on.

Building a Safe Haven: Shelters and Protective Measures

Building a safe haven in the aftermath of a nuclear war is essential for survival. A well-prepared shelter protects you and your loved ones from immediate dangers such as radioactive fallout, extreme weather conditions from nuclear winter, and the breakdown of societal order. In this chapter, we'll explore how to create a functional and secure shelter, the materials and designs that offer the best protection, and the measures needed to sustain life inside.

The primary goal of any post-nuclear shelter is to shield you from radiation. Fallout consists of radioactive particles that settle on the ground and objects after a nuclear explosion. These particles emit dangerous levels of radiation, especially in the first 48 hours when intensity is at its peak. Effective sheltering minimizes exposure to this invisible threat. The key factors in radiation protection are time, distance, and shielding.

If you are fortunate enough to have a pre-existing basement or underground space, this can serve as the foundation for your shelter. The earth provides excellent shielding against gamma rays, which are the most penetrating form of radiation. Ideally, your shelter should be located entirely below ground, with at least three feet of packed earth or dense material like concrete above and around it. If building underground is not an option, the next best choice is a structure with thick, solid walls and no windows or exposed surfaces.

For those constructing a shelter from scratch, simplicity and functionality should guide your design. A trench shelter is a quick and effective option. Dig a trench deep enough to provide substantial coverage, line it with materials like wood or metal for stability, and cover it with heavy-duty plastic sheeting or tarps to prevent water infiltration. Layer the top with dirt, sandbags, or concrete blocks to increase radiation shielding. Ensure the entrance is well-sealed and can be covered with a makeshift door to keep fallout particles out.

If you are using an above-ground space like a room in your home, reinforce it to maximize protection. Select a room in the center of the house, away from external walls and windows. Use furniture, bookshelves, or even filled water containers to create makeshift barriers against radiation. Seal any gaps or cracks with duct tape and plastic sheeting to prevent fallout dust from entering. While not as effective as an underground shelter, this setup can still reduce exposure significantly.

Ventilation is a critical consideration in any shelter. While sealing off the space is necessary to prevent radioactive dust from entering, you must also ensure a supply of fresh air. A manual air filtration system using HEPA filters can help maintain breathable air while keeping contaminants out. If such a system isn't available, create a small air intake and outflow system, ensuring these openings are shielded and positioned away from fallout deposits.

Water and food storage are equally vital. Radiation can contaminate water supplies, so having a stockpile of clean, sealed drinking water is essential. A minimum of one gallon per person per day is recommended, but more is always better. Storing non-perishable food items like canned goods, freeze-dried meals, and energy bars ensures a reliable food supply. Rotate these supplies regularly to keep them fresh.

Lighting and heating are other critical factors for maintaining a livable shelter. Since power grids are unlikely to function, prepare alternative energy sources such as hand-crank lanterns, battery-operated LED lights, or small solar panels. For heating, portable propane heaters can provide warmth, but use them cautiously to avoid carbon monoxide buildup. Blankets, sleeping bags, and layered clothing are essential for staying warm in a cold, dark environment.

Safety goes beyond physical comfort—it's also about securing your shelter against potential threats. Desperate times can lead to desperate behaviors, and you may need to protect yourself from others seeking resources. Reinforce entrances with heavy doors or barricades and consider adding simple alarm systems to alert you to intrusions. Keeping a low profile and avoiding drawing attention to your location can also reduce the likelihood of conflict.

Inside the shelter, organization and sanitation are crucial for maintaining health and morale. Designate specific areas for sleeping, eating, and waste disposal. Use buckets or portable toilets for sanitation, and line them with heavy-duty trash bags for easy disposal. Stock up on hygiene supplies like soap, toothpaste, and disinfectants to reduce the risk of illness.

For long-term sheltering, planning for mental and emotional well-being is as important as physical survival. The confined and stressful conditions of a shelter can take a toll on morale. Bring items like books, games, or musical instruments to provide distractions and maintain a sense of normalcy. If you are with family or a group, establish a routine to give structure to your days and foster cooperation.

Finally, consider the possibility of needing to exit the shelter. Radiation levels decrease over time, but it's essential to monitor them before venturing out. A Geiger counter or dosimeter is invaluable for measuring radiation levels in your environment. Plan for short excursions to gather resources or assess conditions, wearing protective clothing and masks to minimize exposure.

Building a safe haven is not just about creating a physical space—it's about creating a strategy for survival. A well-prepared shelter is a lifeline in the chaos of a post-nuclear world, providing protection, resources, and a foundation for rebuilding. By thinking ahead and taking action, you can increase your chances of enduring the immediate aftermath and emerging into whatever future lies beyond.

Identifying Hot Zones: Where to Avoid and Why

Identifying and avoiding hot zones is critical in the aftermath of a nuclear war. Hot zones refer to areas with high levels of radiation caused by fallout, contaminated materials, or lingering radioactive hotspots. These zones pose immediate and long-term risks to anyone who ventures into them. Knowing where these areas are likely to be and understanding their dangers can mean the difference between life and death.

The first step in identifying hot zones is understanding how fallout behaves. When a nuclear explosion occurs, radioactive materials are ejected into the atmosphere, carried by wind, and eventually deposited back onto the ground. The heaviest fallout particles settle closest to the explosion site, creating a zone of intense radiation. However, lighter particles can travel hundreds or even thousands of miles, spreading contamination far from the detonation point.

Ground zero—the area directly beneath the explosion—is the most dangerous hot zone. Within this area, almost everything is destroyed by the initial blast, heat, and radiation. The radiation levels in this zone are often so high that survival is impossible without specialized protective equipment. Even entering ground zero weeks or months after the explosion can expose you to lethal doses of radiation.

Beyond ground zero, the fallout footprint extends outward, with radiation levels gradually decreasing the farther you go. However, wind patterns, terrain, and weather can create uneven distribution, leading to unexpected hotspots. For example, fallout may accumulate in valleys or low-lying areas where particles settle due to gravity. Urban areas with dense materials like concrete and metal may retain more radiation compared to open fields.

To identify these hot zones, having access to reliable tools like Geiger counters or dosimeters is essential. These devices measure radiation levels in the environment and can help you determine whether an area is safe to enter. If you don't have access to such tools, visual clues and common sense can provide some guidance. Areas that were likely targets for nuclear strikes—such as military bases, government facilities, or major cities—should be avoided altogether. Similarly, regions downwind of these targets are at higher risk of contamination.

Rainfall can exacerbate fallout by washing radioactive particles from the air onto the ground, creating concentrated areas of radiation known as rainout zones. If a nuclear event coincides with heavy rain, the areas beneath these rain clouds may become dangerous hot zones, even if they are far from the initial blast site. Being aware of weather patterns during and after a nuclear event can help you predict where these rainout zones might occur.

Another critical consideration is water contamination. Fallout particles can settle in rivers, lakes, and reservoirs, making these water sources hazardous. Avoid drinking or bathing in open water unless you have a reliable method for testing and purifying it. Groundwater from wells may be safer, but it's essential to ensure that the well is properly sealed and located far from surface contamination.

Buildings and infrastructure can also become hot zones if they trap radioactive particles. Rooftops, for instance, are particularly susceptible to fallout accumulation. If you must enter a building in a fallout area, avoid upper floors and roofs, as radiation levels are likely to be higher there. Additionally, be cautious of areas where dust or debris has accumulated, as these may contain concentrated radioactive particles.

In the days and weeks following a nuclear explosion, radiation levels will decrease as radioactive isotopes decay. However, some isotopes, like cesium-137 and strontium-90, have half-lives of decades, meaning they will remain hazardous for years. This long-term contamination can turn certain areas into permanent hot zones. Agricultural land in these regions will be unusable, and the wildlife that inhabits them may become a source of contamination if consumed.

When planning your movements in a post-nuclear world, always prioritize avoiding hot zones. Maps of fallout distribution, if available, can provide valuable information. If you lack access to maps or radiation detection equipment, err on the side of caution by steering clear of areas you suspect were targeted or heavily affected by fallout. Always plan your routes to minimize exposure, taking the safest, most indirect path to your destination.

If you must traverse a suspected hot zone, take precautions to minimize your exposure. Wear protective clothing that covers as much skin as possible, including gloves, masks, and goggles. Limit the time you spend in the area, and move quickly but carefully to avoid stirring up contaminated dust. Once you exit the zone, decontaminate yourself by removing outer clothing and washing exposed skin thoroughly.

Hot zones are among the greatest hazards in a post-nuclear world, but they are not insurmountable obstacles. By understanding where these areas are likely to be and why they are dangerous, you can make informed decisions that protect you and your loved ones. Knowledge, caution, and preparation are your best defenses against the invisible threats of radiation, allowing you to navigate the aftermath with greater confidence and safety.

The Science of Radioactive Particles: What You Need to Know

Radioactive particles are at the core of the dangers posed by nuclear fallout. Understanding the science behind these particles is essential for survival in a post-nuclear world, as it empowers you to protect yourself and your environment. These particles originate from the materials involved in a nuclear explosion, which undergo a process called radioactive decay. This process releases energy in the form of radiation, which can damage living organisms and contaminate the environment.

When a nuclear bomb detonates, the intense heat and energy of the explosion vaporize materials from the bomb itself, along with the surrounding environment. These materials mix with radioactive isotopes created by the nuclear reaction, forming a cloud of particles that is carried into the atmosphere. As the particles cool, they condense and fall back to Earth, creating fallout.

Radioactive particles emit three main types of radiation: alpha particles, beta particles, and gamma rays. Each type behaves differently and poses unique risks.

Alpha Particles

Alpha particles are relatively large and heavy. They cannot penetrate clothing or human skin, making them less dangerous externally. However, if inhaled, ingested, or absorbed through open wounds, they become a serious threat. Inside the body, alpha particles can damage cells and DNA, leading to illnesses like cancer. Materials containing isotopes like uranium or plutonium often emit alpha particles.

Beta Particles

Beta particles are smaller and more penetrating than alpha particles. They can pass through clothing and damage skin, causing radiation burns. If beta-emitting particles are ingested or inhaled, they can cause internal harm similar to alpha particles. Strontium-90, a common byproduct of nuclear explosions, is a beta emitter that accumulates in bones and poses long-term health risks.

Gamma Rays

Gamma rays are a form of electromagnetic radiation, much like X-rays but far more energetic. They can penetrate most materials, including the human body, causing damage to internal organs and tissues. Gamma rays are particularly dangerous because they are difficult to block without dense materials like lead or thick concrete. Cesium-137 and iodine-131 are common gamma-emitting isotopes found in fallout.

The intensity of radiation emitted by these particles decreases over time, a phenomenon known as radioactive decay. The rate of decay is measured using the concept of half-life—the time it takes for half of a radioactive substance to lose its radioactivity. Some isotopes, like iodine-131, have short half-lives (about eight days), meaning their radiation levels drop relatively quickly. Others, like cesium-137 and strontium-90, have half-lives of around 30 years, posing long-term contamination risks.

The behavior of radioactive particles is influenced by environmental factors such as wind, rain, and terrain. Wind disperses fallout over large areas, with lighter particles traveling farther than heavier ones. Rain can wash fallout out of the atmosphere, creating localized hotspots called rainout zones. Terrain features like valleys or depressions may trap fallout particles, leading to higher concentrations of radiation in these areas.

Radioactive particles can contaminate air, water, soil, and living organisms. In the air, fallout particles can be inhaled, directly exposing lung tissue to radiation. Contaminated water sources become hazardous to drink, while soil contamination affects agriculture by making crops unsafe for consumption. Animals that graze on contaminated plants or drink radioactive water can become carriers of radiation, making their meat and milk dangerous for humans.

To protect yourself from radioactive particles, focus on minimizing exposure through time, distance, and shielding. Time refers to reducing the duration of exposure to radiation. Distance involves staying as far away as possible from radioactive sources, as radiation intensity decreases with distance. Shielding means using materials like lead, concrete, or dense earth to block or absorb radiation.

Decontamination is another vital measure. If you suspect exposure to fallout, remove your outer clothing carefully to avoid spreading radioactive dust. Wash exposed skin with soap and water, paying particular attention to the face, hands, and hair. Contaminated items should be sealed in plastic bags and kept away from living spaces.

Understanding the science of radioactive particles also helps you make informed decisions about food and water safety. Fallout particles can settle on crops and livestock, making them unsafe to consume unless thoroughly tested or decontaminated. Sealed, pre-packaged food and water stored indoors are generally safe. Avoid open water sources like lakes and rivers unless you have tested them for radiation and purified them.

Radiation detection tools like Geiger counters and dosimeters are invaluable in assessing the presence and intensity of radioactive particles. Geiger counters measure radiation levels in the environment, while dosimeters track your cumulative exposure. Learning how to use these devices effectively can help you identify safe areas and avoid dangerous ones.

Radioactive particles are invisible, but their effects are far-reaching and long-lasting. By understanding how they behave and the risks they pose, you can take proactive steps to protect yourself and your environment. Knowledge of the science behind these particles is not just empowering—it is essential for survival in a world altered by nuclear catastrophe.

Staying Clean: Decontamination Techniques for People and Pets

Decontamination is one of the most critical steps for survival in a post-nuclear world. Radioactive fallout particles are invisible to the naked eye, but their presence on your skin, clothes, or in your immediate environment can lead to prolonged exposure to harmful radiation. Learning effective decontamination techniques for yourself, your family, and your pets can significantly reduce your risk of radiation poisoning and other long-term health effects.

The first rule of decontamination is to act quickly but carefully. Once you suspect exposure to fallout, prioritize finding shelter to minimize further exposure. Decontamination should take place inside a sealed environment to prevent additional contamination from the outside.

Decontaminating People

The process begins with removing contaminated clothing, as it often carries the majority of radioactive particles. Carefully peel off your outer garments, turning them inside out as you do to trap fallout particles. Place the clothing in a plastic bag or container, seal it tightly, and move it far from living areas. Avoid shaking the clothes, as this can release particles into the air.

Next, focus on cleaning your body. Start with a thorough rinse using clean, lukewarm water, as it helps to wash away fallout particles without damaging your skin. If water is scarce, use wet wipes or damp cloths, but prioritize the face, hands, and hair, as these areas are most exposed. Soap is highly effective for breaking down and removing contaminants, so use it generously during your wash. Be gentle to avoid creating abrasions where particles could enter the skin.

Pay extra attention to your hair. Use mild shampoo without conditioner, as conditioner can bind radioactive particles to your hair strands. Rinse thoroughly, ensuring all suds and contaminants are washed away. Avoid scrubbing too harshly, as it can damage your scalp and increase the risk of particle absorption.

For open wounds or cuts, take extra precautions. Cover the wound with a clean, waterproof dressing before beginning decontamination to prevent particles from entering. If contamination is suspected on a wound, flush it with clean water or saline and re-dress it with sterile bandages.

Decontaminating Pets

Pets are highly susceptible to fallout contamination due to their fur, which can trap particles. To decontaminate a pet, wear protective gloves and a mask to prevent exposure to particles shaken loose during the process. Start by brushing or wiping down the animal with a damp cloth to remove loose debris. This step is particularly important for long-haired animals, as their fur can hold more fallout.

Next, bathe the animal using clean water and pet-safe shampoo. Work the shampoo into a lather, focusing on areas like the paws, tail, and underbelly where particles are more likely to accumulate. Avoid getting water or soap in the animal's eyes, ears, or nose. Rinse thoroughly, ensuring no soap or contaminants remain.

Dry your pet with a clean towel, taking care to keep them warm in the colder temperatures likely during a nuclear winter. Dispose of all towels, brushes, and water used during the decontamination process in sealed bags to prevent spreading contamination.

Managing Contaminated Items

Contaminated items, including clothing, shoes, and personal belongings, should be handled with care. Place these items in sealed plastic bags or containers and store them far from your living area. If they need to be reused, clean them thoroughly with soapy water and rinse multiple times. Items that cannot be effectively decontaminated, such as porous materials, should be discarded.

Water and Soap Supplies

The effectiveness of decontamination depends heavily on having access to clean water and soap. Stockpiling these essentials before a nuclear event can save lives. If water is limited, prioritize its use for cleaning the most exposed areas, such as the face, hands, and hair. Keep a supply of wet wipes or alcohol-based sanitizers as an alternative for minor decontamination.

Preventing Re-Contamination

After decontamination, maintaining a clean environment is crucial. Seal doors and windows to prevent fallout from entering your shelter. Place doormats or towels at entry points to wipe off shoes and feet, and change them regularly. Designate a specific area for removing outer clothing and shoes to keep fallout away from living spaces.

For pets, create a safe, enclosed area indoors where they can stay until the environment outside is less hazardous. Limit their contact with potentially contaminated surfaces and clean their paws regularly if they must go outside.

Psychological Challenges of Decontamination

The process of decontaminating yourself, loved ones, or pets can be stressful and emotionally draining. The fear of missing a spot or accidentally spreading contamination can heighten anxiety. Take a systematic approach, focusing on one step at a time, and reassure yourself that even partial decontamination significantly reduces the risk of radiation exposure.

Final Thoughts

Staying clean in a radioactive environment is an ongoing effort, not a one-time event. By understanding and practicing effective decontamination techniques, you can protect yourself, your loved ones, and your pets from the hidden dangers of fallout. The key is to remain vigilant, prepared, and methodical in your approach, ensuring that you minimize exposure and create a safe space for recovery and survival.

Testing the Air: Tools and Methods for Measuring Radiation

Testing the air for radiation is a vital step in surviving the aftermath of a nuclear war. Fallout particles released during a nuclear event can contaminate the atmosphere, making it hazardous to breathe or remain exposed. Measuring radiation levels in the air helps you make informed decisions about when it is safe to venture outside, where to travel, and how to protect yourself and your family. In this chapter, we will explore the tools and methods used to test air radiation and how to interpret the results effectively.

Why Testing Air Radiation Matters

After a nuclear explosion, radioactive particles are carried into the atmosphere. These particles emit ionizing radiation, which can cause severe harm if inhaled, ingested, or absorbed through the skin. Airborne particles settle over time, but during the first hours and days after a nuclear event, they pose the greatest threat. Knowing the radiation levels in the air allows you to assess the risk and determine whether it is safe to leave your shelter or undertake necessary activities outdoors.

Tools for Measuring Radiation

Several tools are available for measuring radiation levels in the air, each with its unique features and applications:

- **Geiger Counters**: These devices detect and measure ionizing radiation by counting the number of radioactive particles passing through a tube filled with gas. Geiger counters are portable and relatively easy to use, making them an essential tool for monitoring radiation levels in your surroundings, including the air.
- **Dosimeters**: Dosimeters measure the cumulative dose of radiation exposure over time. While not specifically designed to test air radiation, they provide valuable information about overall exposure and are useful for tracking the safety of individuals in radioactive environments.
- **Air Sampling Devices**: These specialized tools collect air samples for analysis. High-efficiency particulate air (HEPA) filters or paper filters can trap radioactive particles, which can then be tested using a Geiger counter or other radiation-detection equipment.
- **Ion Chambers**: These devices measure the intensity of radiation in the environment by detecting ionization in a chamber filled with air. Ion chambers are particularly useful for assessing gamma radiation levels.
- **Radon Detectors**: While primarily designed to detect radon gas in homes, some models can also provide general radiation readings, offering insight into airborne hazards.

How to Test Air Radiation

Testing air radiation requires proper handling of the equipment and an understanding of the environmental factors affecting radiation levels. Follow these steps to effectively measure air radiation:

1. **Choose the Right Location**
   Conduct tests in an open area where air circulation is representative of the environment. Avoid enclosed spaces, as these may have different radiation levels than the outdoors.
2. **Set Up the Equipment**
   For Geiger counters or dosimeters, ensure the device is calibrated according to the manufacturer's instructions. Place the device at chest or breathing level to measure the air you would typically inhale.

3. **Take Initial Readings**
   Begin by taking baseline readings to understand the current radiation levels. Note the unit of measurement (e.g., millisieverts per hour, microsieverts per hour, or counts per minute) and record the results.
4. **Conduct Air Sampling**
   If using an air sampling device, run the equipment for a specified duration to collect particles on a filter. Afterward, test the filter with a Geiger counter to determine the level of radioactive contamination in the air.
5. **Repeat Measurements**
   Radiation levels in the air can fluctuate due to wind, weather, and the decay of radioactive isotopes. Conduct regular tests to track changes over time and identify patterns.
6. **Interpret the Results**
   Compare the readings to established safety thresholds. Radiation levels below 0.1 microsieverts per hour are generally considered safe for outdoor activity. Levels above this range indicate increased risk, requiring precautions like limiting time outdoors, wearing protective gear, or remaining in a shelter.

Enhancing Accuracy

Environmental factors like wind, rain, and temperature can affect radiation readings. Rain, for example, can temporarily increase ground radiation as it washes fallout from the air, creating localized hotspots. Wind can disperse fallout particles, leading to inconsistent readings. To enhance accuracy:

- Take multiple readings in different locations.
- Test at different times of the day to account for environmental variations.
- Use filters or shielding to distinguish between airborne and ground radiation.

Safety Precautions during Testing

When testing the air for radiation, prioritize your safety:

- Wear protective clothing, including gloves and a mask, to avoid direct contact with radioactive particles.
- Limit your time outside if radiation levels are high.
- Decontaminate yourself and your equipment after testing to prevent bringing radioactive particles into your shelter.

Alternative Methods

If you lack access to advanced equipment, improvisation can provide some insights. For example, placing sticky tape or adhesive sheets in the open air can capture fallout particles. These can then be tested with a Geiger counter. While not as precise as air sampling devices, this method offers a rough estimate of airborne contamination.

Understanding Radiation Decay

Airborne radiation decreases over time as radioactive isotopes decay. The rule of thumb is that radiation intensity drops to 10% of its initial level after 48 hours and continues to decline. Regular testing helps you monitor this decline and make decisions about when it is safe to emerge from shelter.

Practical Applications of Air Testing

Knowing the radiation levels in the air informs key survival decisions, such as:

- When to venture outside for food, water, or supplies.
- Where to relocate if your area becomes too hazardous.
- How to protect yourself with gear like respirators or filters.

Final Thoughts

Testing the air for radiation is an essential skill in a post-nuclear world. The tools and methods described here can help you assess the risks in your environment and take proactive steps to stay safe. By combining technology, knowledge, and vigilance, you can reduce exposure and navigate the dangers of airborne radiation with confidence.

Water Safety: Purification and Storage after Fallout

Water safety becomes a critical concern in the aftermath of a nuclear event. Radioactive fallout can contaminate open water sources, making them unsafe to drink or use. Ensuring access to clean, potable water is essential for survival and long-term health. In this chapter, we'll explore how fallout affects water, methods for purifying contaminated water, and best practices for storing clean water to sustain you and your family in a post-nuclear world.

How Fallout Affects Water

Fallout particles are carried by wind and eventually settle on surfaces, including rivers, lakes, and reservoirs. These particles contain radioactive isotopes, such as iodine-131, cesium-137, and strontium-90, which can dissolve in water or remain suspended as particulate matter. Drinking or using contaminated water can lead to internal exposure to radiation, causing severe health issues, including radiation sickness and increased cancer risk.

Groundwater sources, such as wells, are generally less susceptible to direct fallout contamination because they are protected by layers of soil and rock. However, shallow or improperly sealed wells can still become contaminated if radioactive particles infiltrate the surface. Rainfall after a nuclear event can exacerbate contamination by washing fallout into water sources, creating hotspots of radioactivity.

Prioritizing Safe Water Sources

In the immediate aftermath of a nuclear event, the safest water sources are those that are sealed or protected from fallout. These include:

- Bottled water stored indoors.
- Water from underground wells that are properly sealed.
- Water stored in covered containers or tanks prior to the event.

Avoid using water from open sources such as rivers, lakes, or uncovered tanks unless it has been tested and purified.

Purifying Contaminated Water

If you must use water from a potentially contaminated source, purification is essential. Keep in mind that traditional purification methods, like boiling or chlorination, remove biological contaminants but do not eliminate radioactive particles. Use the following steps to address radioactive contamination:

1. **Settling and Filtering**
   Allow the water to sit undisturbed in a container so that heavy fallout particles settle at the bottom. Carefully pour the clearer water into another container, leaving the sediment behind. Use a fine filter, such as a coffee filter, cloth, or portable water filter, to remove smaller particles.
2. **Ion Exchange Filters**
   Specialized ion exchange filters can reduce certain radioactive isotopes, such as cesium-137 and strontium-90. These filters are often found in advanced water filtration systems or portable survival kits.
3. **Reverse Osmosis**
   Reverse osmosis (RO) systems are highly effective at removing radioactive particles by forcing water through a semi-permeable membrane. While these systems require pressure or electricity, they are among the best

options for long-term purification if resources are available.

4. **Distillation**

   Distillation involves boiling water and collecting the vapor, which leaves most contaminants behind. While effective at removing radioactive particles, it is a resource-intensive process that requires time, fuel, and equipment.

5. **Chemical Treatment**

   Adding specific chemicals, such as potassium iodide, can reduce the absorption of radioactive iodine by the thyroid gland. However, this method addresses only iodine contamination and is not a comprehensive solution for other isotopes.

Testing Water for Radiation

Use a Geiger counter or radiation detector to test water for contamination. Place the detector near the surface of the water and monitor the readings. If the levels are high, avoid using the water, even for washing or irrigation. Keep in mind that some radioactive isotopes may not emit detectable gamma radiation and could still be present.

Storing Clean Water

Once you have access to purified or uncontaminated water, proper storage is essential to prevent recontamination and ensure a steady supply. Follow these guidelines:

- **Use Sealed Containers**: Store water in airtight, food-grade containers. Plastic bottles, jugs, or barrels designed for water storage are ideal.
- **Keep Containers Covered**: Protect stored water from dust, fallout particles, and direct sunlight. Use lids or plastic sheeting to seal open containers.
- **Store in a Cool, Dark Place**: Keep water in a location away from heat and light to prevent microbial growth and degradation of plastic containers.
- **Label and Rotate Supplies**: Mark containers with the date of storage and rotate your supply regularly to ensure freshness. Even treated water can become stale over time.

Managing Limited Water Resources

In a survival situation, water conservation becomes crucial. Use water judiciously for drinking, cooking, and essential hygiene. Avoid waste by repurposing water for multiple uses—for example, using washing water for cleaning non-food items or flushing waste.

Alternative Water Sources

If conventional sources are unavailable, consider harvesting rainwater, melting snow, or extracting moisture from the air using condensation methods. Ensure these sources are tested and purified before use, as they may also be contaminated by fallout.

Long-Term Solutions

For long-term survival, consider installing a reliable water purification system, such as a gravity-fed filter or an RO system powered by alternative energy sources like solar panels. Learning to construct DIY filtration systems using materials like sand, charcoal, and gravel can also be a valuable skill.

The Importance of Staying Hydrated

In the stress of survival, it can be tempting to ration water excessively, but dehydration poses serious health risks. Even in a contaminated environment, properly purified water is better than no water at all. Ensure that everyone in your group drinks enough water to maintain their strength and health.

Final Thoughts

Water is life, even in the direst circumstances. Understanding how fallout affects water, knowing how to purify it, and storing it safely are essential skills for surviving a nuclear aftermath. With the right knowledge and preparation, you can secure clean, safe water for yourself and your loved ones, providing a foundation for resilience and hope in a challenging new world.

Food Contamination: Identifying and Avoiding Tainted Supplies

Food contamination is a major concern in the aftermath of a nuclear event. Radioactive fallout can settle on crops, livestock, and stored food supplies, making them unsafe to consume. Knowing how to identify and avoid contaminated food is crucial for minimizing exposure to harmful radiation. In this chapter, we will explore how fallout affects food, techniques for identifying tainted supplies, and strategies for maintaining a safe and sustainable food source.

How Fallout Contaminates Food

Radioactive fallout consists of tiny particles that can adhere to surfaces, penetrate packaging, and be absorbed by living organisms. Crops, fruits, and vegetables exposed to fallout may carry radioactive particles on their surfaces or absorb isotopes like cesium-137 and strontium-90 from contaminated soil. Livestock grazing on tainted pasture or drinking contaminated water can also accumulate radiation in their tissues, milk, and eggs.

Processed or packaged foods stored outdoors or in unsealed environments may be affected if fallout settles on them or seeps through weak packaging. Even stored food indoors can become contaminated if fallout particles enter the storage area.

Identifying Contaminated Food

Visually inspecting food is not enough to determine whether it is safe, as radioactive particles are invisible and tasteless. However, there are steps you can take to assess the likelihood of contamination:

1. **Location and Exposure**
   Consider where the food was stored or grown. Food grown in open fields, harvested after the fallout, or stored in unsealed areas is more likely to be contaminated. Packaged food stored indoors in sealed containers or under protective coverings is typically safer.
2. **Packaging Integrity**
   Check for signs of compromised packaging, such as holes, tears, or unsealed edges. Fallout particles can enter through these openings and contaminate the contents.
3. **Testing with Radiation Detectors**
   Use a Geiger counter or radiation detector to test food for contamination. Place the device close to the food and monitor the readings. If radiation levels are significantly above the normal background levels, discard the food.
4. **Physical Cleaning**
   For fresh produce, remove the outer layers of leafy greens or peel fruits and vegetables to reduce the risk of contamination. Washing produce with clean, running water and scrubbing with a brush can help remove surface particles, but it will not eliminate isotopes absorbed into the plant.

Avoiding Contaminated Food

The safest strategy is to rely on food that was securely stored or sealed before the fallout. Pre-packaged, canned, or vacuum-sealed foods stored indoors are less likely to be affected. Foods stored in airtight containers or under thick layers of protective material are excellent choices.

- **Canned Goods**: These are among the safest options as they are sealed and impervious to fallout. Wash the exterior of the cans thoroughly before opening to avoid transferring particles to the contents.
- **Dry Goods in Sealed Packaging**: Items like rice, beans, pasta, and grains are safe if their packaging is intact. Transfer them to airtight containers if the original packaging is compromised.
- **Frozen Foods**: Foods in freezers that remained sealed during the fallout may still be safe, though they should be tested or inspected if possible.

Livestock and Animal Products

Meat, milk, and eggs from livestock exposed to fallout can be highly contaminated. Livestock grazing on contaminated grass or drinking tainted water will absorb radioactive isotopes into their tissues. If you must consume animal products, choose those that were stored or processed before the fallout. Boiling milk and thoroughly cooking meat can reduce biological contaminants but will not eliminate radioactive isotopes.

Long-Term Food Strategies

As the immediate fallout danger subsides, focus on creating a sustainable food source:

- **Indoor Gardening**: Grow vegetables and herbs indoors under artificial light using hydroponics or container gardening. This prevents exposure to contaminated soil and water.
- **Soil Remediation**: For outdoor farming, remove and replace the top layers of contaminated soil or treat the soil with techniques like adding clay or potassium to bind and reduce radioactive isotopes.
- **Livestock Management**: If you rely on animals for food, feed them clean, uncontaminated forage or commercially prepared feed stored before the fallout.

Food Testing and Monitoring

Regularly test food sources, including soil and water used for irrigation, with radiation detectors to ensure safety. Keep a record of test results to monitor changes over time as radiation levels decrease.

Hygiene Practices for Handling Food

When handling food in a fallout environment, take precautions to avoid transferring contamination:

- Always wash your hands and utensils with clean water before and after food preparation.
- Use separate cutting boards and knives for produce and animal products.
- Wear gloves when handling potentially contaminated food and dispose of them safely afterward.

Supplementing Diets with Stored Foods

In the immediate aftermath of a nuclear event, stored non-perishable foods will be your primary source of sustenance. Stockpile a variety of nutrient-dense foods like canned meats, beans, vegetables, and fruits to ensure a balanced diet. Include high-calorie items like nuts, peanut butter, and energy bars to meet your daily caloric needs.

The Role of Supplements

Vitamin and mineral supplements can help compensate for dietary deficiencies caused by limited food options. Focus on supplements for essential nutrients like vitamin C, D, calcium, and iodine. Potassium iodide tablets, taken as directed, can protect the thyroid from radioactive iodine exposure.

Mental Preparedness

The scarcity and uncertainty of food safety in a post-nuclear world can lead to anxiety and stress. Maintaining a calm and systematic approach to food management, testing, and preparation will help you navigate this challenge with confidence.

Final Thoughts

Food contamination is a serious but manageable threat in the wake of a nuclear event. By understanding how fallout affects food, taking precautions to identify and avoid contaminated supplies, and implementing long-term food strategies, you can protect yourself and your family from unnecessary exposure. Careful planning and vigilance will ensure that your food remains a source of strength and sustenance in the challenging days ahead.

Growing a New Eden: Safe Gardening in a Contaminated World

In a post-nuclear world, growing your own food becomes a critical part of long-term survival. However, the challenge lies in cultivating crops in an environment potentially contaminated with radioactive fallout. Gardening in such conditions requires careful planning, innovative techniques, and an understanding of how to mitigate contamination risks. In this chapter, we'll explore how to establish a safe and sustainable garden to grow clean, edible crops, creating a new Eden amid adversity.

Understanding Soil Contamination

Radioactive fallout can settle on the surface of the soil, where it can contaminate crops directly or be absorbed by plants through their roots. Isotopes like cesium-137 and strontium-90 are particularly problematic because they mimic essential nutrients such as potassium and calcium, allowing them to enter the food chain.

The degree of soil contamination depends on several factors, including the amount of fallout, the type of soil, and environmental conditions. Clay-rich soils tend to bind radioactive particles more tightly, reducing their availability to plants, while sandy soils allow contaminants to move more freely. Testing your soil for radiation levels before planting is crucial to ensure it is safe for gardening.

Choosing a Safe Location

Selecting the right site for your garden is the first step. If possible, choose an area that was shielded from direct fallout, such as land covered by trees, buildings, or thick layers of snow during the nuclear event. Avoid low-lying areas where runoff water might have concentrated fallout particles.

If no uncontaminated land is available, consider raised beds or container gardening to isolate your crops from the ground. These methods allow you to control the growing medium and reduce the risk of contamination.

Testing and Remediating Soil

Use a Geiger counter or soil testing kit to measure radiation levels. If contamination is present, soil remediation techniques can help reduce its impact:

1. **Topsoil Removal**: Remove and safely dispose of the top few inches of soil, where fallout particles are most likely to have settled.
2. **Soil Amendment**: Add clean materials like clay, biochar, or potassium fertilizers to bind radioactive isotopes and reduce their uptake by plants.
3. **Crop Barriers**: Place a layer of clean soil or mulch over contaminated ground to create a buffer between the crops and radioactive particles.

Choosing the Right Crops

Certain crops are more resistant to absorbing radiation than others. Root vegetables like carrots, radishes, and potatoes are more likely to accumulate contaminants, while fruiting plants like tomatoes, cucumbers, and peppers tend to be safer. Leafy greens like spinach and lettuce can absorb fallout particles that settle on their surfaces but are less likely to take up isotopes from the soil.

Consider growing fast-maturing crops, as shorter growing cycles reduce the time plants are exposed to contamination. Additionally, nutrient-dense crops like kale, beans, and sweet potatoes provide maximum sustenance with minimal space and resources.

Implementing Safe Gardening Techniques

To minimize the risk of contamination, adopt practices that protect your crops and growing environment:

- **Raised Beds**: Build raised garden beds filled with clean soil or compost. This isolates plants from potentially contaminated ground and allows for better control over soil conditions.
- **Mulching**: Apply a thick layer of mulch to the soil surface to prevent fallout particles from coming into contact with your crops.
- **Covering Plants**: Use row covers, plastic sheeting, or greenhouse structures to shield plants from airborne particles and rain that could wash fallout onto them.

Watering Wisely

Water sources may also be contaminated, so it's important to use clean water for irrigation. Rainwater collected after the fallout period may be safe if tested and filtered. Otherwise, rely on sealed, stored water or a well-protected groundwater source. Avoid watering plants with surface water from lakes or rivers unless you've confirmed it is free of contamination.

Harvesting and Preparing Crops

Even with precautions, some surface contamination on crops is possible. To ensure safety, follow these steps during harvest and preparation:

- Wash all produce thoroughly with clean, running water to remove surface particles.
- Peel root vegetables and discard outer leaves of greens to reduce the risk of ingesting radioactive isotopes.
- Test harvested crops with a radiation detector, if available, to confirm they are safe to eat.

Indoor Gardening and Hydroponics

If outdoor gardening is not viable, indoor gardening offers a safer alternative. By growing plants in a controlled environment, you can avoid exposure to contaminated soil and air. Hydroponic systems, which grow plants in nutrient-rich water without soil, are particularly effective in this context.

For indoor gardening, use artificial lighting like LED grow lights to simulate sunlight, and ensure proper ventilation to maintain healthy growing conditions. Crops like herbs, leafy greens, and small fruiting plants are well-suited for indoor cultivation.

Long-Term Sustainability

Building a sustainable garden in a post-nuclear world involves planning for the long haul. Save seeds from your harvest to ensure a continuous supply of plants. Choose heirloom or open-pollinated varieties, which are better suited for seed saving than hybrids. Establish composting systems to recycle organic waste into nutrient-rich soil amendments, reducing dependence on external inputs.

Psychological Benefits of Gardening

Gardening is not just about survival—it can also provide a sense of purpose and normalcy in an otherwise chaotic world. Tending to plants, watching them grow, and reaping the rewards of your labor can be profoundly therapeutic, helping to alleviate stress and maintain mental health.

Final Thoughts

Creating a new Eden in the shadow of nuclear fallout is no small task, but it is a vital one. By understanding the challenges, employing safe gardening techniques, and fostering resilience, you can grow clean, nourishing food even in a contaminated world. With determination and ingenuity, your garden can become a symbol of hope and renewal, proving that life can flourish even in the most challenging circumstances.

Livestock in the Fallout: Raising Animals for Safe Consumption

Raising livestock in a post-nuclear world presents unique challenges, as animals are susceptible to the same dangers of radiation and fallout as humans. Ensuring that your livestock remains safe for consumption requires careful planning, protective measures, and ongoing monitoring to prevent contamination of both the animals and the food products they provide. In this chapter, we will explore how fallout affects animals, strategies for raising livestock safely, and ways to test and protect their meat, milk, and eggs.

Understanding How Fallout Affects Livestock

Radioactive fallout contaminates the environment, including the air, soil, and water that livestock depend on for survival. Animals can be exposed to radiation in several ways:

- **Inhalation**: Breathing in airborne radioactive particles.
- **Ingestion**: Consuming contaminated food or water.
- **Direct Contact**: Fallout particles settling on their skin, fur, or feathers.

Once radioactive isotopes enter an animal's body, they can accumulate in tissues such as muscle, bone, or organs. For example, cesium-137 mimics potassium and can be found in muscle tissue, while strontium-90 behaves like calcium and accumulates in bones and milk.

Choosing Suitable Livestock

Certain types of livestock are better suited for survival and productivity in a fallout-affected environment. Animals with smaller sizes and shorter lifespans, such as chickens, rabbits, or goats, are less likely to accumulate significant levels of radiation compared to larger, longer-lived animals like cows or pigs.

- **Chickens**: Provide eggs and meat with relatively low space and resource requirements.
- **Rabbits**: Grow quickly and offer a steady supply of lean meat.
- **Goats**: Produce milk and meat and are hardy animals that adapt well to challenging conditions.
- **Ducks and Quail**: Alternative poultry options that are efficient and resilient.

Shelter and Protection

The best way to protect livestock from fallout is to provide adequate shelter that minimizes their exposure to radioactive particles:

- **Enclosed Barns or Coops**: Keep animals indoors in a sealed, ventilated structure. Use plastic sheeting or tarps to cover openings and prevent fallout from entering.
- **Raised Floors**: Elevate livestock enclosures to prevent contact with contaminated soil or water.
- **Filtered Ventilation**: Install filters to remove radioactive particles from the air entering the shelter.
- **Decontamination Areas**: Set up designated areas to clean animals and equipment before they enter or leave the shelter.

If outdoor grazing is unavoidable, rotate animals between clean areas and monitor soil and vegetation for contamination.

Feeding Livestock Safely

Contaminated feed is a major pathway for radiation exposure in livestock. To reduce this risk:

- **Stockpile Clean Feed**: Store hay, grains, and other feed in sealed, indoor containers before a nuclear event.
- **Grow Indoor Fodder**: Use hydroponic or indoor gardening techniques to produce fresh, uncontaminated feed.
- **Avoid Contaminated Pastures**: Prevent animals from grazing on land exposed to fallout until it has been tested and deemed safe.

Water sources must also be free from contamination. Provide livestock with clean, stored water or water drawn from deep, sealed wells.

Monitoring and Testing Livestock

Regular testing of livestock and their products is essential to ensure safety. Use radiation detection equipment to monitor animals, feed, and water:

- **Geiger Counters**: Test animal enclosures, feed, and water for radiation hotspots.
- **Testing Milk and Eggs**: Check milk and eggs for radioactive isotopes using laboratory kits or professional services.
- **Observation**: Monitor animals for signs of radiation sickness, such as lethargy, loss of appetite, or unusual health issues.

If contamination is detected, isolate affected animals and avoid consuming their products.

Decontaminating Livestock

Animals exposed to fallout can be decontaminated to reduce radiation levels:

- **Bathing**: Wash animals with clean water and mild soap to remove fallout particles from their skin or fur. Focus on areas where particles are most likely to accumulate, such as the legs, underbelly, and snout.
- **Brushing Feathers or Fur**: Use soft brushes to remove particles from poultry or furry animals.
- **Dietary Adjustments**: Feed animals supplements like potassium or calcium to reduce the absorption of radioactive isotopes like cesium-137 and strontium-90.

Processing and Preparing Livestock Products

If livestock is raised in an area with any risk of contamination, extra precautions must be taken when processing their products:

- **Meat**: Trim away fat and remove bones, as radioactive isotopes often concentrate in these areas. Cook meat thoroughly to destroy biological contaminants, though this does not eliminate radiation.
- **Milk**: Boiling milk does not remove radioactive isotopes, but filtering and testing before consumption can

help identify risks.

- **Eggs**: Wash eggs thoroughly to remove surface contamination before cooking or consuming.

Long-Term Livestock Management

As the immediate fallout danger subsides, focus on creating a sustainable and safe livestock operation:

- **Soil Remediation**: Treat contaminated pastures with clean soil, clay, or other amendments to reduce radiation absorption by plants and grazing animals.
- **Controlled Breeding**: Raise new generations of animals in protected environments to ensure their safety and productivity.
- **Alternative Protein Sources**: Consider supplementing your diet with fish or insects raised in controlled environments as a backup to livestock.

Psychological and Emotional Benefits

Raising animals provides more than food—it offers a sense of purpose and normalcy in a world disrupted by nuclear catastrophe. Tending to livestock, observing their growth, and enjoying their products can foster resilience and hope.

Final Thoughts

Livestock can be a vital resource in a post-nuclear world, but raising them safely requires diligence, preparation, and ongoing monitoring. By understanding the risks, implementing protective measures, and testing animals and their products regularly, you can ensure a steady supply of safe, nutritious food. With care and ingenuity, your livestock operation can thrive, becoming a cornerstone of your survival strategy and a beacon of resilience in challenging times.

The Invisible Enemy: How Radioactive Particles Spread

Radioactive particles, often referred to as fallout, are one of the most insidious threats in the aftermath of a nuclear event. These particles are nearly invisible to the naked eye but have the power to contaminate air, water, soil, and living organisms. Understanding how radioactive particles spread and behave is crucial for minimizing exposure and protecting yourself and your environment.

The Nature of Radioactive Particles

When a nuclear explosion occurs, it releases vast amounts of energy that vaporize materials in its immediate vicinity. These vaporized materials mix with radioactive isotopes generated during the explosion, forming microscopic particles. The size of these particles varies, with larger particles settling closer to the blast site and smaller particles traveling great distances.

These particles emit ionizing radiation, which can damage living cells and tissues. They are classified into alpha particles, beta particles, and gamma rays, each with unique properties:

- **Alpha particles** are large and heavy but can be blocked by skin or clothing. However, they are extremely dangerous if inhaled or ingested.
- **Beta particles** are smaller and can penetrate skin to a certain extent, causing burns and tissue damage.
- **Gamma rays** are highly penetrating and can travel through most materials, including the human body, making them the most harmful form of radiation.

How Fallout Spreads

Radioactive particles can spread through various mechanisms, including atmospheric dispersion, weather patterns, and human activity. The key factors influencing their movement include:

1. Atmospheric Dispersion

After a nuclear explosion, the mushroom cloud carries radioactive particles into the upper atmosphere. Wind currents then disperse these particles over vast areas. The height of the cloud and the strength of the winds determine how far the particles travel.

2. Weather Patterns

Weather conditions play a significant role in fallout distribution. Rain and snow can wash particles out of the atmosphere, creating localized hotspots of radiation known as "rainout zones." These areas are especially hazardous because the concentration of radioactive particles is higher.

3. Surface Contamination

As fallout particles settle, they contaminate surfaces like soil, buildings, vegetation, and water sources. Heavier particles fall first and remain closer to the explosion site, while lighter particles can remain airborne for longer periods.

4. Runoff and Waterways

Rain and melting snow can carry fallout particles into rivers, lakes, and reservoirs. This not only contaminates water sources but also spreads radiation downstream, affecting areas far from the blast site.

5. Human and Animal Activity

People and animals can unknowingly spread radioactive particles through movement and contact. Fallout particles can cling to clothing, shoes, and fur, spreading contamination to clean areas.

Environmental Hotspots

Certain areas are more prone to becoming fallout hotspots due to their geography or weather conditions. These include:

- **Valleys and Depressions**: Fallout particles can accumulate in low-lying areas due to gravity and runoff.
- **Urban Areas**: Buildings, roads, and other infrastructure can trap and concentrate particles.
- **Wetlands and Water Bodies**: Fallout particles can settle in water and be absorbed by aquatic ecosystems.

Detecting the Invisible Threat

Because radioactive particles are invisible and odorless, detection tools are essential for identifying their presence:

- **Geiger Counters**: Measure radiation levels in the environment and help identify contaminated areas.
- **Dosimeters**: Track cumulative radiation exposure over time, providing an indication of personal safety.
- **Air and Water Sampling Kits**: Test for radioactive particles in the air or water to assess contamination levels.

Minimizing Exposure

The best way to protect yourself from radioactive particles is to minimize exposure through time, distance, and shielding:

- **Time**: Limit the duration of exposure to contaminated areas.
- **Distance**: Stay as far away as possible from fallout zones or hotspots.
- **Shielding**: Use barriers like concrete, lead, or dense materials to block radiation.

Preventing Particle Spread

To prevent the spread of radioactive particles into your living space:

- **Seal Shelter Openings**: Use duct tape and plastic sheeting to seal windows, doors, and ventilation systems.
- **Decontaminate Clothing**: Remove and dispose of outer clothing worn in contaminated areas, and wash exposed skin thoroughly.
- **Control Foot Traffic**: Set up decontamination zones at entrances to prevent particles from being tracked indoors.

Long-Term Behavior of Fallout

Over time, the intensity of radiation from fallout decreases due to the decay of radioactive isotopes. This process, known as radioactive decay, is measured in half-lives—the time it takes for half of a substance's radioactivity to dissipate. Some isotopes, like iodine-131, decay quickly, while others, like cesium-137 and strontium-90, remain hazardous for decades.

Despite this decay, fallout particles can become embedded in soil and water, posing long-term risks. Contaminated areas may remain unsafe for agriculture, habitation, or wildlife for years or even centuries.

Practical Applications of Knowledge

Understanding how radioactive particles spread helps you:

- **Identify Safe Zones**: Use wind patterns, geography, and weather data to locate areas less likely to be contaminated.
- **Plan Evacuations**: Avoid areas downwind of the blast or those prone to rainout.
- **Maintain Clean Environments**: Implement strict hygiene and decontamination protocols to reduce secondary exposure.

Final Thoughts

Radioactive particles are an invisible enemy that can infiltrate every aspect of your environment, from the air you breathe to the water you drink. By understanding how these particles spread and taking proactive measures to limit their impact, you can navigate the dangers of a fallout-affected world with confidence and resilience. Knowledge, vigilance, and preparedness are your greatest tools in facing this silent but deadly threat.

Protecting Your Family from Radiation Exposure

Protecting your family from radiation exposure is one of the most critical priorities in a post-nuclear world. Radiation exposure can cause immediate health risks, long-term complications, and even generational effects. By understanding the dangers of radiation, implementing protective measures, and fostering a vigilant, proactive approach, you can safeguard your family's well-being in a fallout-contaminated environment.

Understanding Radiation Exposure

Radiation affects the body by damaging cells and DNA, leading to symptoms ranging from mild to life-threatening. Acute radiation syndrome (ARS), or radiation sickness, occurs when someone is exposed to high doses of radiation over a short period. Symptoms include nausea, vomiting, fatigue, and, in severe cases, organ failure. Long-term exposure to lower levels of radiation increases the risk of cancer and genetic mutations.

Radiation exposure can occur in three main ways:

1. **External Exposure**: From gamma rays or beta particles penetrating the body.
2. **Inhalation**: Breathing in radioactive particles suspended in the air.
3. **Ingestion**: Consuming contaminated food or water.

Building a Safe Environment

Creating a safe living space is your first line of defense against radiation exposure. This involves selecting and fortifying a shelter, reducing contact with radioactive particles, and controlling the air quality.

1. **Choose the Right Shelter**:
    - Underground shelters or basements are ideal because the earth provides natural shielding.
    - Reinforce above-ground shelters with thick materials like concrete, brick, or packed earth to block gamma rays.

1. **Seal the Shelter**:
    - Use plastic sheeting, duct tape, and weather stripping to seal windows, doors, and ventilation points to prevent fallout particles from entering.
    - Regularly inspect and maintain seals to ensure they remain effective.

1. **Air Filtration**:
    - Install HEPA filters to remove radioactive particles from the air.
    - Use manual or battery-powered ventilation systems to circulate clean air if electricity is unavailable.

1. **Radiation Shielding Inside**:
    - Create an inner safe zone within your shelter using additional shielding like lead sheets, sandbags, or even stacks of books and furniture.

Personal Protective Measures

Minimizing direct exposure to radiation is crucial when venturing outside or handling contaminated materials.

1. **Protective Clothing**:
    ○ Wear long sleeves, pants, gloves, and boots to cover as much skin as possible.
    ○ Use masks or respirators to avoid inhaling radioactive particles.
2. **Decontamination**:
    ○ Remove and seal outer clothing before re-entering the shelter.
    ○ Wash exposed skin and hair with soap and water to remove fallout particles.
3. **Limiting Time Outside**:
    ○ Spend as little time as possible in areas with known contamination.
    ○ Monitor radiation levels with a Geiger counter or dosimeter before and during excursions.

Ensuring Clean Food and Water

Contaminated food and water are significant sources of internal radiation exposure. Protect your family by prioritizing safe sources and thorough testing.

1. **Food Safety**:
    ○ Consume only sealed, pre-packaged foods stored indoors before the fallout.
    ○ Wash and peel fresh produce, and avoid items grown outdoors unless they've been tested for radiation.
2. **Water Safety**:
    ○ Use stored or sealed water supplies. Test and purify any water collected from open sources.
    ○ Avoid using rainwater until it has been filtered and confirmed safe.
3. **Testing and Monitoring**:
    ○ Use radiation detectors to test food and water regularly.
    ○ Keep records of test results to track changes in safety over time.

Protecting Vulnerable Family Members

Children, pregnant women, and elderly family members are more susceptible to the effects of radiation due to their developing or weakened immune systems. Special precautions include:

1. **Shielding Children**:
    ○ Assign the safest areas of the shelter to children and ensure they have limited exposure to contaminated zones.
    ○ Keep their activities confined to clean spaces.
2. **Supporting Pregnant Women**:
    ○ Provide additional shielding and a clean environment to minimize risks to both mother and fetus.
    ○ Ensure a nutrient-rich diet to counteract the effects of radiation.
3. **Caring for the Elderly**:
    ○ Monitor health closely and provide access to medical supplies for chronic conditions.
    ○ Reduce physical strain to minimize exposure risks.

Educating and Preparing Your Family

Knowledge is a powerful tool in protecting against radiation. Educate your family on safety measures and establish routines to ensure everyone knows what to do in an emergency.

1. **Radiation Basics**:
   - Teach family members to recognize safe and unsafe areas, as well as the signs of radiation sickness.
2. **Emergency Drills**:
   - Practice evacuation and sheltering procedures to ensure everyone is familiar with the steps to take.
3. **Assign Roles**:
   - Assign specific responsibilities, such as monitoring radiation levels or managing food and water supplies, to ensure efficiency and shared accountability.

Monitoring Health

Radiation exposure can cause delayed symptoms, so regular health monitoring is essential.

1. **Watch for Symptoms**:
   - Be alert for nausea, fatigue, skin burns, or unusual changes in health that could indicate radiation sickness.
   - Seek medical help if possible, and isolate affected individuals to reduce secondary risks.
2. **Use Dosimeters**:
   - Equip each family member with a dosimeter to track cumulative radiation exposure.
   - Rotate duties that involve higher exposure to minimize risks.
3. **Maintain a Medical Kit**:
   - Stock a kit with iodine tablets, anti-nausea medication, wound care supplies, and any required prescription medications.

Psychological Well-Being

The stress and fear of living in a radioactive environment can take a toll on mental health. Maintaining a positive and supportive atmosphere is vital.

1. **Foster Normalcy**:
   - Create routines, assign tasks, and incorporate leisure activities to provide a sense of structure and purpose.
2. **Communicate Openly**:
   - Encourage family members to share their concerns and feelings.
   - Offer reassurance and focus on actionable steps to maintain a sense of control.
3. **Provide Comfort Items**:
   - Include familiar or comforting items like toys for children, books, or games to reduce stress.

Protecting your family from radiation exposure requires preparation, vigilance, and adaptability. By creating a safe environment, practicing proper hygiene, ensuring clean food and water, and fostering a supportive atmosphere, you can shield your loved ones from the invisible dangers of fallout. Knowledge and proactive measures are your greatest allies in navigating the challenges of a nuclear aftermath, ensuring the safety and resilience of your family in uncertain times.

Radiation and Health: Long-term Effects and Coping Strategies

The long-term effects of radiation exposure are a sobering reality in the aftermath of a nuclear event. While immediate health impacts like radiation sickness dominate the early stages, exposure to even low levels of radiation over time can lead to chronic health problems, genetic damage, and psychological strain. Understanding these long-term effects and developing coping strategies is crucial for maintaining health and quality of life in a fallout-contaminated world.

How Radiation Affects the Body

Radiation exposure damages cells by ionizing molecules within them, disrupting normal biological functions. The extent of the damage depends on the dose, duration, and type of radiation. Key long-term effects include:

1. **Increased Cancer Risk**:
   - Radiation exposure increases the likelihood of developing cancers, particularly leukemia, thyroid cancer, and breast cancer. These risks are higher for those exposed to significant doses of radiation, though even low-level exposure over time can contribute.
2. **Cardiovascular Issues**:
   - Chronic radiation exposure may lead to cardiovascular problems, including heart disease and stroke, due to damage to blood vessels and heart tissues.
3. **Genetic Damage**:
   - Radiation can cause mutations in DNA, which may be passed on to future generations. These genetic effects are a significant concern for pregnant women and those planning families.
4. **Immune System Suppression**:
   - Prolonged exposure can weaken the immune system, leaving individuals more susceptible to infections and illnesses.
5. **Cataracts and Vision Problems**:
   - Radiation can accelerate the development of cataracts, leading to impaired vision over time.
6. **Fertility Issues**:
   - High doses of radiation can harm reproductive organs, reducing fertility in both men and women.

Coping with the Physical Effects

Managing long-term health effects involves a combination of preventative measures, medical care, and lifestyle adjustments:

1. **Regular Health Monitoring**:
   - Schedule routine health checks to identify and address early signs of radiation-related illnesses.
   - Use dosimeters to track cumulative radiation exposure over time.
2. **Cancer Screening**:
   - Prioritize screening for cancers commonly linked to radiation exposure, such as thyroid and breast cancer. Early detection significantly improves treatment outcomes.
3. **Diet and Nutrition**:
   - A diet rich in antioxidants, vitamins, and minerals helps repair cellular damage and boost the immune system. Include foods high in vitamin C, E, selenium, and beta-carotene.
   - Iodine-rich foods, such as seaweed, can help protect the thyroid gland, particularly if consumed

before or shortly after exposure to radioactive iodine.

4. **Medical Interventions**:
    - Potassium iodide (KI) tablets protect the thyroid from radioactive iodine exposure. These should only be taken under guidance and are not effective against other isotopes.
    - Chelation therapy can help remove certain radioactive isotopes from the body, though it is not effective for all types of radiation.
5. **Protective Lifestyle**:
    - Minimize further exposure by avoiding contaminated areas and using protective gear when necessary.
    - Practice good hygiene, including regular decontamination, to reduce ongoing contact with radioactive particles.

Addressing Psychological Impacts

The stress of living with radiation exposure and its potential health effects can take a toll on mental health. Coping strategies include:

1. **Staying Informed**:
    - Knowledge reduces fear. Understand the risks and the steps you can take to mitigate them.
    - Avoid misinformation and rely on credible sources for updates on radiation levels and safety measures.
2. **Building a Support Network**:
    - Connect with others facing similar challenges. Sharing experiences and coping strategies fosters a sense of community and resilience.
3. **Stress Management**:
    - Incorporate relaxation techniques like meditation, deep breathing, or yoga into daily routines to reduce anxiety.
    - Set aside time for leisure activities, hobbies, and moments of joy to maintain emotional balance.
4. **Counseling and Therapy**:
    - Seek professional mental health support if feelings of fear, sadness, or hopelessness become overwhelming.
    - Family counseling can help address the collective emotional strain and strengthen relationships.

Supporting Vulnerable Groups

Certain populations, such as children, pregnant women, and the elderly, are more vulnerable to the long-term effects of radiation exposure:

1. **Children**:
    - Their growing bodies absorb radiation more readily, increasing risks of developmental and long-term health issues.
    - Ensure they receive regular medical checkups and maintain a diet rich in essential nutrients.
2. **Pregnant Women**:
    - Radiation can harm fetal development, leading to birth defects or developmental delays. Extra precautions, including shielding and avoiding contaminated areas, are necessary.

3. **Elderly Individuals**:
    ◦ Weakened immune systems and pre-existing health conditions may exacerbate the effects of radiation. Provide them with tailored medical care and monitoring.

Long-Term Environmental Considerations

The environment plays a crucial role in mitigating long-term radiation risks:

1. **Soil and Water Testing**:
    ◦ Regularly test soil and water for contamination and use remediation techniques where necessary to reduce radiation levels.
2. **Safe Food Practices**:
    ◦ Grow crops in raised beds or controlled environments like greenhouses to avoid contamination.
    ◦ Test harvested food regularly for radioactive isotopes.
3. **Rebuilding Safe Communities**:
    ◦ Prioritize resettlement in areas with low radiation levels. Advocate for decontamination efforts in affected zones.

Planning for the Future

While the long-term effects of radiation exposure are daunting, planning for the future helps foster hope and resilience:

1. **Education and Skill Development**:
    ◦ Learn new skills in sustainable living, agriculture, or medicine to adapt to a changed world.
    ◦ Teach younger generations about radiation safety and self-sufficiency.
2. **Technological Solutions**:
    ◦ Invest in and advocate for research on radiation mitigation technologies and treatments.
3. **Cultural and Emotional Resilience**:
    ◦ Preserve traditions, stories, and art to maintain a sense of identity and purpose amidst adversity.

Final Thoughts

The long-term effects of radiation exposure are serious but not insurmountable. By understanding the risks, adopting proactive health measures, and fostering emotional resilience, you can protect yourself and your family while adapting to the challenges of a post-nuclear world. The road ahead may be difficult, but with knowledge, preparation, and determination, it is possible to thrive and rebuild in the face of adversity.

Medical Preparedness: Treating Radiation Wounds and Poisoning

Medical preparedness is essential for surviving the aftermath of a nuclear event. Radiation wounds and poisoning can cause immediate and long-term health complications, and access to professional medical care may be limited. Understanding how to identify, treat, and manage radiation-related injuries ensures you are equipped to care for yourself and your family in such an environment. In this chapter, we'll explore practical steps to address radiation wounds and poisoning, along with the supplies and knowledge needed for effective medical preparedness.

Recognizing Radiation Wounds and Poisoning

Radiation exposure affects the body in different ways, depending on the dose and duration of exposure. Immediate and visible injuries are often accompanied by systemic effects.

1. **Radiation Burns**:
   - Caused by high doses of radiation, these burns may resemble severe sunburn and appear within hours or days of exposure.
   - Symptoms include redness, blistering, peeling, and, in severe cases, ulceration.
2. **Acute Radiation Syndrome (ARS)**:
   - Occurs after exposure to high doses of radiation and affects rapidly dividing cells in the body.
   - Symptoms progress in phases:
     - **Prodromal Stage**: Nausea, vomiting, diarrhea, and fatigue appear within hours.
     - **Latency Period**: Symptoms may temporarily subside, giving a false sense of recovery.
     - **Manifest Illness Phase**: Symptoms worsen, including hair loss, fever, infections, bleeding, and organ failure.
3. **Delayed Effects**:
   - Chronic health problems like anemia, infertility, or cancer may develop months or years after exposure.

Treating Radiation Wounds

Radiation wounds, such as burns or cuts contaminated with radioactive particles, require careful handling to prevent further damage or infection.

1. **Decontamination**:
   - Gently rinse wounds with clean, lukewarm water to remove radioactive particles.
   - Use mild soap and avoid scrubbing, as this can aggravate tissue damage.
   - Cover the wound with a sterile, waterproof dressing to prevent further contamination.
2. **Pain Management**:
   - Use over-the-counter pain relievers like ibuprofen or acetaminophen to reduce discomfort.
   - Cool compresses may alleviate swelling and pain for burns.
3. **Infection Control**:
   - Apply antibiotic ointment to prevent infections in minor wounds.
   - For deeper wounds, clean thoroughly and seek antibiotics if available.
4. **Monitoring**:
   - Watch for signs of infection, such as redness, swelling, pus, or fever, and treat promptly.

Treating Radiation Poisoning

Managing radiation poisoning involves reducing the body's radioactive burden and addressing the symptoms.

1. **Reducing Absorption**:
   - Administer potassium iodide (KI) tablets immediately after exposure to block radioactive iodine from being absorbed by the thyroid gland. These are most effective within the first 24 hours.
   - Chelating agents, such as Prussian blue or calcium-DTPA, can bind to certain radioactive isotopes (e.g., cesium-137 or plutonium) and help the body excrete them. These require medical guidance.
2. **Symptom Management**:
   - Combat dehydration caused by vomiting and diarrhea with oral rehydration solutions or electrolyte-rich fluids.
   - Use anti-nausea medications like ondansetron or over-the-counter options such as ginger or motion sickness remedies.
3. **Immune System Support**:
   - Radiation damages bone marrow, reducing white blood cell production and increasing infection risk. Boost immunity with a nutrient-rich diet, focusing on vitamins A, C, E, and zinc.
4. **Monitoring**:
   - Track symptoms and progression. If severe fatigue, persistent vomiting, or bleeding occurs, prioritize rest and hydration.

Essential Medical Supplies

A well-stocked medical kit is invaluable for treating radiation-related injuries and illnesses. Include the following:

- **Decontamination Supplies**:
  - Soap, water, disposable gloves, and masks.
- **Wound Care**:
  - Sterile gauze, adhesive bandages, waterproof dressings, antiseptic wipes, and antibiotic ointment.
- **Medications**:
  - Potassium iodide tablets, pain relievers, anti-nausea medications, and antibiotics.
- **Hydration and Nutrition**:
  - Oral rehydration salts, electrolyte tablets, and multivitamins.
- **Radiation Detection Tools**:
  - Geiger counter, dosimeter, or personal radiation monitor.
- **Miscellaneous Supplies**:
  - Scissors, tweezers, disposable syringes, and a thermometer.

Creating a Medical Plan

In addition to supplies, having a clear medical plan helps ensure swift and effective treatment.

1. **Prioritize Decontamination:**
   - Always address decontamination first to prevent further exposure and spread of radioactive particles.

1. **Triage Care:**
   - Assess injuries and symptoms to determine the severity. Treat life-threatening issues, like severe dehydration or infection, first.
2. **Isolation for Contaminated Individuals:**
   - If a family member shows signs of radiation poisoning, isolate them in a designated area to minimize the risk of spreading particles.
3. **Record Keeping:**
   - Document symptoms, treatments, and radiation exposure levels for each person. This information helps track recovery and identify long-term health risks.

Psychological Support

Medical preparedness includes addressing the emotional impact of injuries and radiation exposure:

1. **Provide Reassurance:**
   - Stay calm and offer emotional support to reduce stress and anxiety for the injured person.
2. **Maintain Communication:**
   - Discuss treatment steps openly and involve family members in care decisions.
3. **Focus on Recovery:**
   - Encourage rest and a positive outlook to aid physical healing.

Preparing for Long-Term Care

Radiation-related injuries and illnesses may require ongoing care:

1. **Cancer Screening:**
   - Regularly monitor for symptoms of radiation-induced cancers, particularly thyroid, leukemia, and skin cancers.
2. **Chronic Conditions:**
   - Address long-term effects like infertility, cardiovascular issues, or weakened immunity with appropriate medical interventions.
3. **Community Support:**
   - Seek support from local communities or organizations if professional medical care becomes available.

Final Thoughts

Medical preparedness is a cornerstone of survival in a fallout-contaminated world. By equipping yourself with the knowledge, supplies, and skills needed to treat radiation wounds and poisoning, you can protect your family and promote recovery in the face of daunting challenges. While the risks are significant, proactive care and a calm, methodical approach can make a profound difference in long-term health and survival.

Surviving the Cold: Strategies for the Nuclear Winter

Surviving a nuclear winter—a period of prolonged cold, darkness, and environmental disruption caused by a large-scale nuclear war—requires careful planning, adaptability, and resourcefulness. With temperatures dropping drastically due to the blockage of sunlight by soot and ash in the atmosphere, food shortages, energy scarcity, and psychological strain become significant challenges. This chapter explores practical strategies for enduring the cold and surviving in a world transformed by nuclear winter.

Understanding Nuclear Winter

Nuclear winter occurs when large quantities of smoke and soot from nuclear explosions and resulting firestorms are propelled into the upper atmosphere. These particles block sunlight, lowering temperatures worldwide. This phenomenon disrupts agriculture, alters weather patterns, and creates a harsh environment similar to an extended, extreme winter. The severity and duration depend on the scale of the conflict, with effects potentially lasting months or years.

Creating a Warm Shelter

The first step in surviving nuclear winter is securing a shelter that provides protection from the cold and insulation against radiation.

1. **Location Matters**:
   - Underground shelters or basements are ideal for maintaining stable temperatures.
   - If underground options aren't available, choose a room in the center of your home with no external walls to minimize heat loss.
2. **Insulation**:
   - Reinforce walls, windows, and doors with blankets, plastic sheeting, or additional layers of cardboard to trap heat.
   - Use rugs, carpets, or straw on floors for added insulation.
3. **Heating Sources**:
   - Use portable propane or kerosene heaters for warmth, but ensure proper ventilation to avoid carbon monoxide poisoning.
   - Wood-burning stoves are effective but require a steady supply of fuel and proper chimney maintenance.
   - For areas without fuel, body heat, candles, and thermal blankets can provide warmth.
4. **Light and Heat Retention**:
   - Cover windows with heavy curtains or blankets to keep warmth inside.
   - Cluster family members together in one room to concentrate body heat.

Conserving Energy and Resources

With fuel and electricity likely to be scarce, conservation becomes critical.

1. **Maximize Daylight**:
   - Use natural light during the day to save on fuel and batteries for lighting.
   - Create reflectors from aluminum foil to amplify available light.
2. **Layer Clothing**:
   - Dress in multiple layers, including thermal undergarments, wool sweaters, and insulated outerwear.
   - Hats, gloves, and socks are essential for retaining body heat.
3. **Sleeping Arrangements**:
   - Use sleeping bags rated for extreme cold and layer blankets for additional warmth.
   - Sleep in close proximity to others to share heat.
4. **Preserve Fuel**:
   - Use fuel sparingly and prioritize heating during the coldest parts of the day.
   - Insulate water pipes and food storage areas to reduce the need for heating.

Food and Nutrition

Food scarcity during nuclear winter is a major concern, as crops fail and supply chains break down. Maintaining proper nutrition is essential for energy and immunity.

1. **Stockpile Non-Perishables**:
   - Store canned goods, grains, dried beans, nuts, and freeze-dried meals.
   - Rotate your stockpile to prevent spoilage and ensure freshness.
2. **Grow Indoor Food**:
   - Use hydroponics or container gardening with artificial light to grow fast-maturing crops like sprouts, microgreens, or herbs.
3. **Ration Wisely**:
   - Plan meals to provide balanced nutrition while conserving supplies.
   - Avoid overeating; the body requires fewer calories in a sedentary, insulated environment.
4. **Supplement with Vitamins**:
   - Keep a supply of multivitamins to compensate for limited access to fresh produce.

Water Management

Access to clean water is crucial, especially as natural water sources may freeze or become contaminated.

1. **Prevent Freezing**:
   - Store water in insulated containers or underground to protect it from freezing temperatures.
   - Rotate water supplies to prevent ice buildup.
2. **Purify Water**:
   - Boil, filter, or chemically treat water to ensure safety before consumption.
3. **Melt Snow Safely**:
   - Collect and melt snow for drinking water, but boil it to remove contaminants.

Psychological Resilience

The psychological toll of nuclear winter is immense. Isolation, prolonged darkness, and survival stress can affect mental health.

1. **Maintain a Routine**:
    - Establish a daily schedule to provide structure and a sense of purpose.
    - Include time for physical activity, even if it's simple exercises indoors.
2. **Stay Connected**:
    - Foster communication and teamwork among family members to reduce feelings of isolation.
    - If possible, use radios to connect with other survivors.
3. **Engage the Mind**:
    - Keep morale high with games, books, or hobbies.
    - Create rituals or traditions to mark time and celebrate small victories.

Long-Term Adaptation

Planning for long-term survival involves creating systems that sustain life as the effects of nuclear winter gradually recede.

1. **Renewable Energy**:
    - Invest in wind turbines, hand-crank generators, or solar panels if sunlight levels improve.
    - Use these energy sources to power lighting, heating, and small appliances.
2. **Rebuild Food Supplies**:
    - As temperatures rise, prepare for outdoor gardening by testing soil for radiation and using clean, remediated land.
    - Raise hardy livestock, such as chickens or rabbits, for food and manure.
3. **Monitor the Environment**:
    - Use radiation detectors to assess when it's safe to expand activities outdoors.
    - Test air, water, and soil regularly as contamination levels decrease.

Final Thoughts

Surviving a nuclear winter demands ingenuity, resourcefulness, and determination. By prioritizing warmth, food, water, and mental health, you can endure the harsh conditions and lay the groundwork for recovery. Though the world may seem bleak, every step you take to adapt and thrive brings you closer to a new chapter of resilience and renewal.

Mental Health in the Apocalypse: Coping with Trauma

Mental health becomes as critical as physical survival in the aftermath of a nuclear apocalypse. Coping with trauma, grief, fear, and uncertainty while managing the stress of daily survival is a monumental challenge. Yet, resilience and mental fortitude can mean the difference between enduring and succumbing to the pressures of this new reality. This chapter explores strategies for maintaining mental health and fostering emotional well-being in a world turned upside down.

Understanding Trauma and Stress in a Post-Nuclear World

The psychological impact of a nuclear event is profound and multifaceted. Survivors face numerous stressors, including the loss of loved ones, the destruction of familiar surroundings, and the daily battle for basic necessities. Common psychological responses include:

1. **Acute Stress Reactions:**
   - Symptoms like shock, confusion, irritability, and difficulty concentrating are normal in the immediate aftermath.
2. **Post-Traumatic Stress Disorder (PTSD):**
   - Flashbacks, nightmares, hypervigilance, and emotional numbness may develop over time as the brain struggles to process the event.
3. **Survivor's Guilt:**
   - Feelings of guilt for surviving when others did not can weigh heavily on individuals.
4. **Chronic Stress:**
   - The ongoing demands of survival, isolation, and uncertainty about the future contribute to prolonged stress and fatigue.

Building Emotional Resilience

Emotional resilience is the ability to adapt to adversity and recover from stress. Strengthening this quality can help individuals and families cope with the challenges of a post-nuclear world.

1. **Accepting the New Reality:**
   - Acknowledge the magnitude of the situation without dwelling on what has been lost.
   - Focus on what you can control, such as immediate survival needs and fostering connections.
2. **Maintaining Perspective:**
   - Remind yourself that difficult circumstances are temporary and that small steps toward recovery can lead to significant progress.
3. **Practicing Gratitude:**
   - Find moments to appreciate what remains—whether it's your family, a warm meal, or the ability to adapt and survive.
4. **Creating Purpose:**
   - Set achievable goals, such as organizing your shelter, growing food, or helping others. Purpose gives life meaning even in dire circumstances.

Daily Practices for Mental Well-Being

Incorporating daily practices to nurture mental health can help alleviate stress and foster a sense of normalcy.

1. **Establish a Routine**:
   - Structure your days with regular activities like preparing meals, maintaining your shelter, and engaging in recreation. Routines provide predictability and reduce anxiety.
2. **Physical Activity**:
   - Even limited movement, such as stretching or walking within your shelter, can boost mood and alleviate stress by releasing endorphins.
3. **Mindfulness and Relaxation**:
   - Practice deep breathing, meditation, or visualization exercises to calm the mind and reduce feelings of overwhelm.
   - Focus on the present moment rather than dwelling on the past or worrying about the future.
4. **Creative Outlets**:
   - Engage in activities like drawing, writing, or crafting. Expressing emotions through creativity can be therapeutic and help process trauma.
5. **Laughter and Play**:
   - Find humor and moments of joy, whether through storytelling, playing games, or reminiscing. Laughter can be a powerful antidote to stress.

Supporting Family and Community

Strong relationships provide a foundation for emotional support and collective resilience.

1. **Open Communication**:
   - Encourage family members to share their thoughts and feelings without fear of judgment.
   - Listen actively and validate each person's experience, even if you don't have solutions.
2. **Foster Teamwork**:
   - Assign roles and responsibilities to each family member, fostering a sense of contribution and teamwork.
3. **Provide Comfort**:
   - Small gestures, like a comforting word, a warm drink, or a shared moment of quiet, can strengthen bonds and soothe emotions.
4. **Connect with Others**:
   - If possible, maintain contact with other survivors through radios, letters, or in-person visits. Community connections reduce isolation and foster hope.

Addressing Specific Mental Health Challenges

Certain psychological conditions require targeted coping strategies:

1. **Managing Anxiety**:
   - Break tasks into manageable steps to avoid feeling overwhelmed.
   - Practice grounding techniques, like focusing on your surroundings or naming objects in the room, to calm panic.

2. **Dealing with Grief**:
    ◦ Allow yourself to mourn the loss of loved ones, familiar places, and the life you once knew. Suppressing grief can delay healing.
3. **Combatting Depression**:
    ◦ Stay engaged with daily activities and avoid isolating yourself from others.
    ◦ Seek out moments of beauty or meaning, even in small ways, to rekindle hope.
4. **Helping Children Cope**:
    ◦ Provide reassurance and stability for children, answering their questions honestly while offering hope.
    ◦ Use play and storytelling to help them process their emotions and fears.

Finding Hope in the Apocalypse

Maintaining hope in the face of adversity is one of the most powerful tools for psychological survival. Hope inspires action, builds resilience, and strengthens the will to endure.

1. **Focus on Small Victories**:
    ◦ Celebrate every achievement, no matter how minor—whether it's growing food, solving a problem, or making it through another day.
2. **Visualize a Better Future**:
    ◦ Picture the life you want to rebuild and the steps you'll take to get there. A positive vision can inspire determination and perseverance.
3. **Find Meaning in Survival**:
    ◦ Reflect on what you've learned and how you've grown through adversity. Emphasize the importance of resilience and adaptability.

Accessing Professional Support

If professional mental health resources become available, take advantage of them:

1. **Therapy and Counseling**:
    ◦ Speaking with a trained professional can help you process trauma and develop coping strategies.
2. **Group Support**:
    ◦ Join or form support groups to share experiences and foster mutual encouragement.
3. **Medical Interventions**:
    ◦ Seek medical help if severe anxiety, depression, or PTSD symptoms persist, and medication may be an option if available.

Final Thoughts

The psychological toll of a nuclear apocalypse is immense, but resilience, connection, and hope can help you navigate the darkness. By addressing mental health proactively and fostering emotional strength, you can endure the trauma, adapt to the new reality, and find moments of light even in the shadow of catastrophe. Survival is as much about the mind as it is about the body—and nurturing both is essential for a better tomorrow.

Understanding Radiation Levels: The Tools to Measure Exposure

Understanding radiation levels and knowing how to measure exposure are critical skills in a post-nuclear world. Radiation is invisible, tasteless, and odourless, making it impossible to detect without specialized tools. Accurately assessing radiation levels in your environment, food, water, and personal exposure can help you make informed decisions to protect yourself and your family. This chapter explores the tools available for measuring radiation, how they work, and practical applications in a survival context.

Why Measure Radiation?

Radiation is emitted by radioactive isotopes, which decay over time, releasing energy in the form of ionizing radiation. Exposure to this radiation can damage cells, leading to immediate health effects like radiation sickness and long-term risks like cancer. Measuring radiation helps you:

1. Determine the safety of your environment.
2. Assess contamination in food, water, and other resources.
3. Monitor personal exposure to ensure it remains within safe limits.
4. Decide when it is safe to leave a shelter or enter previously contaminated areas.

Key Concepts in Radiation Measurement

To understand radiation levels, it's important to familiarize yourself with key concepts and units:

1. **Types of Radiation**:
    - **Alpha particles**: Heavy and slow; dangerous if inhaled or ingested but blocked by clothing or skin.
    - **Beta particles**: Smaller and more penetrating; can damage skin and internal tissues.
    - **Gamma rays**: Highly penetrating; pose the greatest external hazard.
2. **Units of Measurement**:
    - **Sieverts (Sv)**: Measures the biological effect of radiation on the body.
    - **Grays (Gy)**: Measures the absorbed dose of radiation by matter.
    - **Counts per Minute (CPM)**: Indicates the number of radiation particles detected per minute.
3. **Radiation Thresholds**:
    - **Natural Background Radiation**: 0.1–0.2 microsieverts per hour (μSv/h) is typical.
    - **Safe Exposure Levels**: Prolonged exposure above 1 mSv/year increases health risks.
    - **Dangerous Levels**: Acute exposure above 1 Sv can cause radiation sickness.

Tools for Measuring Radiation

Several devices can detect and measure radiation, each suited for specific tasks:

1. **Geiger Counters**:
    - **Purpose**: Measure radiation levels in the environment and objects.
    - **How It Works**: Detects ionizing particles passing through a gas-filled tube, producing an audible click or visual reading.
    - **Applications**: Check contamination in food, water, and surrounding areas.

2. **Dosimeters**:
   - **Purpose**: Measure cumulative radiation exposure over time.
   - **How It Works**: Tracks total dose received by an individual, often displayed in microsieverts or millisieverts.
   - **Applications**: Monitor personal exposure during outdoor activities or near suspected hotspots.
3. **Radiation Survey Meters**:
   - **Purpose**: Provide detailed measurements of radiation levels.
   - **How It Works**: Similar to a Geiger counter but more sensitive and precise.
   - **Applications**: Assess radiation intensity for professional or detailed analysis.
4. **Air Sampling Devices**:
   - **Purpose**: Measure airborne radioactive particles.
   - **How It Works**: Draws air through a filter to collect particles, which are then tested with a radiation detector.
   - **Applications**: Evaluate indoor and outdoor air safety.
5. **Radiation Alert Cards**:
   - **Purpose**: Provide a simple, low-tech indication of radiation presence.
   - **How It Works**: Changes color when exposed to radiation.
   - **Applications**: Quick and portable but less precise.
6. **Personal Radiation Monitors**:
   - **Purpose**: Portable devices worn on the body to track individual exposure.
   - **How It Works**: Provides real-time readings and cumulative dose information.
   - **Applications**: Useful for ongoing activities in areas with potential contamination.

How to Measure Radiation

Using radiation detection tools effectively requires proper handling and interpretation:

1. **Calibrate Devices**:
   - Follow the manufacturer's instructions to ensure accuracy.
   - Test the device in a low-radiation environment to establish baseline readings.
2. **Test the Environment**:
   - Use a Geiger counter to scan your shelter, surrounding area, and suspected hotspots.
   - Move slowly and cover a wide area to get comprehensive readings.
3. **Check Food and Water**:
   - Place the detector close to the surface of food or water containers.
   - For water, test both the liquid and any sediment that may have settled.
4. **Monitor Personal Exposure**:
   - Wear a dosimeter or personal radiation monitor to track cumulative exposure.
   - Note readings regularly and adjust activities to minimize risk.
5. **Assess Time and Distance**:
   - Radiation levels decrease with distance from the source and over time.
   - Use measurements to determine when it is safe to leave shelter or approach a contaminated area.

Interpreting Radiation Levels

Understanding the readings from your device is essential for making informed decisions:

- **Low Levels**:
    - Readings near background levels (0.1–0.2 μSv/h) are safe for normal activities.
- **Elevated Levels**:
    - Persistent exposure above 1 μSv/h should prompt caution; limit time in such areas.
- **High Levels**:
    - Readings above 10 μSv/h are hazardous and require immediate action to reduce exposure.

Practical Applications

Radiation measurement tools are indispensable for a range of survival tasks:

1. **Shelter Safety**:
    - Test your shelter for radiation leaks or hotspots.
2. **Travel and Exploration**:
    - Assess outdoor areas for safety before venturing out.
3. **Resource Testing**:
    - Check soil, water, and food for contamination.
4. **Community Monitoring**:
    - Share data with others to map safe zones and dangerous areas.

Maintenance and Limitations

To ensure reliability, maintain your radiation detection tools:

- **Battery Management**:
    - Stockpile spare batteries and test devices regularly.
- **Shielding and Damage**:
    - Protect devices from moisture, dust, and physical damage.
- **Limitations**:
    - Some isotopes may not emit detectable gamma radiation, requiring additional testing methods.

Final Thoughts

Radiation measurement tools are vital for navigating the invisible dangers of a post-nuclear world. By mastering their use and understanding how to interpret readings, you can protect yourself and your loved ones from unnecessary exposure. Knowledge is power, and in the face of radiation, it can be the key to survival.

Fallout Myths and Facts: Separating Truth from Fiction

In the chaos and uncertainty of a nuclear event, misinformation can spread as quickly as fear. Separating myths from facts about nuclear fallout is essential for making informed decisions and protecting yourself and your family. Misunderstandings about radiation, fallout, and survival strategies can lead to unnecessary risks or false confidence. In this chapter, we'll debunk common myths about nuclear fallout and explain the facts you need to know to stay safe.

Myth 1: Radiation Is Instantly Fatal

Fact: The effects of radiation depend on the dose, type, and duration of exposure. While high doses of radiation can cause immediate harm or death, low-level exposure over time may result in long-term health risks, such as cancer. Acute radiation sickness (ARS) occurs only at doses significantly higher than natural background radiation, and survival often depends on prompt medical intervention and minimizing further exposure.

Myth 2: All Fallout Is Equally Dangerous

Fact: Fallout particles vary in their radioactive potency and longevity. Some isotopes, like iodine-131, decay quickly (half-life of about 8 days) and pose a short-term risk. Others, like cesium-137 and strontium-90, have half-lives of 30 years, creating long-term hazards in the environment. Understanding the types of isotopes present and their behavior is crucial for assessing danger levels.

Myth 3: You Can See or Smell Radiation

Fact: Radiation is invisible, tasteless, and odorless. The only way to detect and measure it is with specialized tools like Geiger counters, dosimeters, or radiation survey meters. Any visible signs, such as dust or ash, are fallout particles that may contain radioactive material, but the radiation itself cannot be detected without equipment.

Myth 4: Boiling Water Removes Radiation

Fact: Boiling water can kill biological contaminants, like bacteria, but it does not remove radioactive isotopes. To make water safe, use filtration methods that trap particles or chemical treatments that bind certain isotopes, such as ion exchange resins. Distillation is also effective, as it separates radioactive contaminants from water vapor.

Myth 5: Staying Indoors Is Always Safe

Fact: While indoor sheltering reduces exposure to fallout, the effectiveness of your shelter depends on its construction and location. A well-sealed underground shelter with thick walls provides excellent protection, while a wooden house with open windows offers little shielding. To improve safety, seal gaps, reinforce walls, and use additional shielding materials.

Myth 6: A Nuclear Explosion Wipes Out All Life

Fact: While the immediate vicinity of a nuclear explosion suffers catastrophic damage, areas farther away may remain habitable after fallout levels decrease. The effects of a nuclear event depend on factors like the bomb's size, altitude, and the number of explosions. With proper preparation and knowledge, survival is possible even in affected regions.

Myth 7: Fallout Is Only a Short-Term Threat

Fact: While the most intense radiation from fallout occurs in the first 48 hours, some isotopes remain hazardous for decades. Areas heavily contaminated by cesium-137 or strontium-90, for instance, may be unsafe for farming or habitation for years. Long-term monitoring and remediation are required to mitigate these risks.

Myth 8: Radiation Exposure Makes You Glow

Fact: This trope comes from science fiction and has no basis in reality. Radiation exposure does not cause people or objects to glow. Visible glowing sometimes associated with radiation in media is due to specific materials, like radium paint, or phenomena like Cherenkov radiation, which occurs only in specialized conditions.

Myth 9: Fallout Shelters Are Expensive and Impractical

Fact: While elaborate fallout shelters can be costly, effective protection doesn't require a high-tech facility. A simple basement reinforced with sandbags, earth, or concrete, combined with proper sealing and ventilation, provides significant shielding. Affordable materials and creative solutions can make shelters accessible to most people.

Myth 10: Once Fallout Settles, It's Harmless

Fact: Fallout particles remain radioactive even after settling on surfaces. These particles can be stirred up by wind, water, or human activity, leading to renewed exposure. Proper decontamination of surfaces, clothing, and equipment is essential to avoid secondary contamination.

Myth 11: Only Urban Areas Are at Risk

Fact: While cities and military targets are primary strike zones, fallout can spread far beyond these areas, carried by wind and weather. Rural regions downwind of a nuclear explosion may experience significant contamination, making preparedness crucial no matter where you live.

Myth 12: Lead Suits or Radiation Pills Offer Total Protection

Fact: While lead is an effective barrier against gamma rays, lead suits are impractical for everyday use and do not protect against alpha or beta particles. Potassium iodide (KI) tablets protect the thyroid from radioactive iodine but do not shield against other isotopes or types of radiation. Comprehensive protection requires a combination of sheltering, decontamination, and monitoring.

Myth 13: You Can Survive by Digging a Hole and Covering It

Fact: A basic trench can provide temporary protection against fallout, but long-term survival requires adequate ventilation, insulation, and access to clean food and water. Improvised shelters need to be carefully constructed to provide sufficient shielding and prevent collapse.

Myth 14: Radiation Is Contagious

Fact: Radiation itself cannot spread from one person to another. However, fallout particles can cling to clothing, skin, and hair, potentially contaminating others. Decontamination is essential to prevent the spread of radioactive particles.

Myth 15: Fallout Will Kill Everything Outdoors

Fact: While fallout can harm plants and animals, its impact depends on the level of contamination. Some areas may experience severe damage, while others recover more quickly. Hardy crops and livestock raised in protected conditions can survive and even thrive in less-affected areas.

Fact-Based Survival Strategies

By separating fact from fiction, you can focus on practical measures to protect yourself and your family:

1. **Understand Radiation Decay**:
   - Radiation levels drop significantly over time, with 90% of radioactivity decreasing within seven days. Plan your activities accordingly.
2. **Use Reliable Tools**:
   - Equip yourself with radiation detectors and understand how to interpret their readings.
3. **Shelter Effectively**:
   - Build a well-sealed and insulated shelter with adequate ventilation and shielding materials.
4. **Practice Decontamination**:
   - Remove fallout particles from surfaces, clothing, and skin to reduce exposure.
5. **Educate Yourself and Others**:
   - Knowledge is the best defense against both radiation and misinformation.

Final Thoughts

In a world filled with uncertainty, understanding the facts about nuclear fallout empowers you to make informed decisions and take effective action. By debunking myths and embracing evidence-based strategies, you can increase your chances of survival and resilience in the face of adversity. Knowledge is your greatest ally in the fight against the invisible dangers of radiation.

Radioactive Soil: Challenges and Solutions for Safe Cultivation

Radioactive soil is one of the most pressing challenges in a post-nuclear world, as contamination affects the safety of crops and livestock raised on affected land. Fallout particles that settle into the soil can persist for years or even decades, posing long-term risks to food production and human health. Safe cultivation in radioactive soil requires understanding the nature of contamination, its risks, and strategies to mitigate or eliminate its effects. This chapter explores these challenges and provides solutions for reclaiming soil for safe agricultural use.

Understanding Soil Contamination

Radioactive soil contamination occurs when fallout particles settle on the ground. These particles can either remain on the surface or penetrate deeper layers over time due to rain, wind, and human activity. The extent of contamination depends on the type and concentration of radioactive isotopes in the fallout.

1. **Key Isotopes in Soil**:
   - **Cesium-137**: Mimics potassium, absorbed by plants and accumulates in edible parts. Half-life: ~30 years.
   - **Strontium-90**: Mimics calcium, accumulates in plants, animals, and human bones. Half-life: ~29 years.
   - **Iodine-131**: Short-lived but highly dangerous for immediate contamination. Half-life: ~8 days.
2. **Spread of Contamination**:
   - **Surface Contamination**: Fallout particles adhere to the soil surface, directly contaminating crops.
   - **Absorption**: Radioactive isotopes dissolve in water and are absorbed into the soil, where they bind to minerals and organic matter.
   - **Runoff and Deposition**: Rain and erosion can move contaminated soil particles to new locations, affecting previously clean areas.

Risks of Cultivating in Radioactive Soil

1. **Crop Contamination**:
   - Plants absorb radioactive isotopes through their roots, particularly if the isotopes mimic essential nutrients like potassium or calcium.
   - Leafy greens and root vegetables are especially vulnerable to surface contamination.
2. **Livestock Exposure**:
   - Animals grazing on contaminated pastures or consuming feed grown in radioactive soil accumulate isotopes in their tissues, milk, and eggs.
3. **Human Health Hazards**:
   - Consuming contaminated crops or animal products can lead to internal radiation exposure, increasing the risk of cancer and other health issues.

Testing and Assessing Soil

Before attempting cultivation, it's critical to test and assess the level of soil contamination.

1. **Radiation Detection Tools**:
   - Use Geiger counters or radiation survey meters to measure the intensity of gamma radiation in the soil.
   - Portable spectrometers can identify specific isotopes present in the contamination.
2. **Sampling and Lab Testing**:
   - Collect soil samples from different depths and locations to determine the concentration of radioactive isotopes.
   - Professional lab analysis provides detailed information about contamination levels and types.
3. **Mapping Contamination**:
   - Create a contamination map of your land to identify hotspots and safer areas for cultivation.

Solutions for Safe Cultivation

Addressing radioactive soil contamination requires a combination of mitigation, remediation, and alternative farming techniques.

1. Soil Remediation Techniques

- **Topsoil Removal**:
  - Remove and safely dispose of the top layer of soil where contamination is concentrated.
  - Replace with clean soil from uncontaminated areas.
- **Plowing and Mixing**:
  - Deep plowing can dilute surface contamination by mixing it with less-contaminated lower layers.
  - While this reduces surface radiation levels, it may spread contamination within the soil.
- **Binding Agents**:
  - Add materials like clay, zeolite, or biochar to the soil to bind radioactive isotopes, preventing their uptake by plants.
  - Potassium fertilizers can reduce cesium-137 absorption, while calcium-based additives can counteract strontium-90.
- **Phytoremediation**:
  - Grow specific plants, such as sunflowers or mustard greens, that absorb radioactive isotopes. These plants can then be harvested and safely disposed of to reduce contamination levels.

2. Protective Cultivation Methods

- **Raised Beds**:
  - Use clean soil in raised beds to isolate crops from contaminated ground.
  - Line the beds with plastic or impermeable barriers to prevent leaching from the underlying soil.
- **Greenhouses**:
  - Enclose crops in greenhouses filled with clean soil to shield them from contaminated air, soil, and water.

- **Hydroponics:**
    - ○ Grow plants in nutrient-rich water without soil, eliminating the risk of soil-based contamination.
    - ○ Ensure the water source is clean and free of radioactive particles.

3. Crop Selection

- **Choose Safer Crops:**
    - ○ Fruiting plants like tomatoes, peppers, and squash absorb fewer radioactive isotopes than leafy greens or root vegetables.
    - ○ Avoid growing crops known to accumulate isotopes, such as spinach or potatoes, in moderately contaminated soil.
- **Fast-Growing Crops:**
    - ○ Opt for crops with shorter growing cycles, as they spend less time absorbing isotopes from the soil.

Managing Long-Term Risks

1. **Soil Monitoring:**
    - ○ Regularly test soil radiation levels to track changes over time and identify when areas become safe for cultivation.
2. **Crop Testing:**
    - ○ Use radiation detectors to test harvested crops for contamination before consumption.
3. **Safe Disposal:**
    - ○ Dispose of contaminated plant material and topsoil safely, following guidelines for handling radioactive waste.
4. **Rotational Farming:**
    - ○ Alternate planting locations to limit prolonged exposure of crops to contaminated soil.

Psychological and Community Considerations

Addressing radioactive soil contamination requires collaboration and resilience:

1. **Education and Training:**
    - ○ Teach family members or community groups about soil safety, testing methods, and cultivation techniques.
2. **Sharing Resources:**
    - ○ Pool resources like clean soil, seeds, and equipment to support collective farming efforts.
3. **Psychological Support:**
    - ○ Focus on the long-term benefits of remediation and celebrate small victories to maintain morale.

Final Thoughts

Radioactive soil presents a significant obstacle to agriculture, but it is not an insurmountable one. Through careful testing, innovative techniques, and ongoing remediation efforts, it is possible to grow food safely even in challenging conditions. With patience, knowledge, and adaptability, you can reclaim contaminated land and lay the foundation for a sustainable, resilient future.

Protecting the Vulnerable: Caring for Children and the Elderly

Caring for children and the elderly in a post-nuclear world presents unique challenges, as these groups are especially vulnerable to the effects of radiation, malnutrition, stress, and illness. Children's developing bodies and immune systems make them more susceptible to radiation exposure and its long-term consequences. Similarly, the elderly often face reduced physical resilience, pre-existing health conditions, and psychological stress. This chapter focuses on strategies to protect, nurture, and support these at-risk groups to ensure their survival and well-being.

Why Children and the Elderly Are More Vulnerable

1. **Children**:
   - Their smaller bodies absorb more radiation relative to their size.
   - Developing organs and tissues are more sensitive to radiation's effects, increasing the risk of growth delays, cancers, and thyroid disorders.
   - Their psychological and emotional needs can be heightened by fear and confusion.
2. **Elderly**:
   - Pre-existing health conditions, such as cardiovascular disease or weakened immune systems, reduce their ability to withstand stress and illness.
   - Slower recovery from injuries or illnesses.
   - Increased susceptibility to dehydration and malnutrition.

General Principles of Care

1. **Prioritize Safety**:
   - Shield children and the elderly from exposure to radiation by ensuring they remain in well-sealed, insulated shelters.
   - Assign the safest, most comfortable areas of the shelter for their use.
2. **Maintain Cleanliness**:
   - Prevent contamination by enforcing strict hygiene protocols, including decontamination after venturing outside.
   - Ensure clean food, water, and clothing.
3. **Provide Emotional Support**:
   - Address fear and anxiety with reassurance, routines, and emotional connection.
   - Create a sense of normalcy with activities, familiar items, and comforting rituals.

Specific Strategies for Children

1. **Physical Protection**:
   - Use appropriately sized masks or respirators to protect them from inhaling radioactive particles.
   - Ensure their clothing covers as much skin as possible when outside or in potentially contaminated areas.
2. **Nutrition and Hydration**:
   - Provide nutrient-dense foods to support growth and immunity, such as protein-rich meals, fruits, and vegetables when available.

- Monitor hydration carefully, especially during periods of stress or illness.
3. **Education and Engagement**:
   - Teach children basic safety measures in an age-appropriate way, such as staying indoors or washing hands.
   - Engage them in educational or creative activities to keep their minds occupied and reduce anxiety.
4. **Routine Medical Care**:
   - Monitor for signs of radiation exposure, such as nausea, fatigue, or skin changes, and act swiftly if symptoms appear.
   - Include multivitamins and supplements to prevent deficiencies caused by limited diets.
5. **Emotional and Psychological Care**:
   - Be honest but gentle about the situation to build trust while avoiding unnecessary fear.
   - Use storytelling, games, and art to help children express their feelings and cope with stress.

Specific Strategies for the Elderly

1. **Physical Comfort**:
   - Provide warm bedding, clothing, and easily accessible seating to minimize physical strain.
   - Use mobility aids, such as canes or walkers, to prevent falls and injuries.
2. **Manage Pre-existing Conditions**:
   - Stock essential medications and administer them on schedule.
   - Monitor chronic conditions, such as high blood pressure or diabetes, and adapt diets or routines to manage symptoms.
3. **Prevent Isolation**:
   - Include the elderly in group activities and decisions to maintain a sense of purpose and connection.
   - Check in frequently to address physical or emotional needs.
4. **Adapt Diets**:
   - Provide foods that are easy to chew and digest, such as soups, stews, or pureed meals, while ensuring they meet nutritional requirements.
   - Encourage frequent small meals to prevent malnutrition.
5. **Mental Health Support**:
   - Be patient and attentive to signs of depression or anxiety.
   - Share stories, memories, and discussions to create a positive, engaging environment.

Shared Care Practices

1. **Safe Spaces**:
   - Create designated areas within the shelter where children and the elderly can rest, play, or relax without exposure to hazards.
2. **Health Monitoring**:
   - Keep detailed records of each individual's health, symptoms, and treatments to identify patterns or emerging issues.
3. **Regular Hygiene**:
   - Assist with bathing, handwashing, and grooming to maintain cleanliness and prevent illness.
   - Ensure they wear clean, decontaminated clothing.

4. **Activity and Movement**:
    - ◦ Encourage gentle physical activity to prevent stiffness and maintain circulation. For children, this can be playful movement; for the elderly, stretching or light exercise.

Addressing Emotional and Psychological Needs

Both children and the elderly require emotional care to thrive in challenging conditions:

1. **Children**:
    - ◦ Provide reassurance and consistency through routines.
    - ◦ Allow space for play, creativity, and laughter to foster resilience.
2. **Elderly**:
    - ◦ Engage them in storytelling or memory-sharing to provide emotional relief.
    - ◦ Foster a sense of purpose by involving them in age-appropriate tasks, such as teaching or caregiving.
3. **Both Groups**:
    - ◦ Use physical affection, like hugs or hand-holding, to provide comfort.
    - ◦ Share small moments of joy, such as celebrating milestones or enjoying a shared activity.

Special Considerations for Medical Emergencies

1. **Children**:
    - ◦ Act swiftly to address dehydration, fever, or infections, as children's conditions can deteriorate rapidly.
    - ◦ Administer child-sized doses of medications as needed, following medical guidelines.
2. **Elderly**:
    - ◦ Monitor for slow-healing wounds, respiratory issues, or sudden changes in cognitive function, which could indicate underlying problems.
    - ◦ Keep first aid supplies readily available and tailored to common conditions like arthritis or skin irritation.

Preparing for Long-Term Care

Caring for children and the elderly over months or years requires foresight and adaptability:

1. **Resource Planning**:
    - ◦ Stockpile age-appropriate supplies, such as diapers for infants or assistive devices for elderly family members.
2. **Skill Sharing**:
    - ◦ Teach children basic survival skills and involve the elderly in passing down knowledge, creating a sense of empowerment for both.
3. **Community Support**:
    - ◦ If safe, collaborate with other families or groups to pool resources and share caregiving responsibilities.

Final Thoughts

Protecting the most vulnerable members of your family requires compassion, vigilance, and adaptability. By addressing their unique physical and emotional needs, you can provide a foundation for resilience and well-being. Children and the elderly offer hope and wisdom in difficult times—caring for them ensures not just survival, but the preservation of humanity's future.

Waterborne Radiation: Risks in Rivers, Lakes, and Oceans

Waterborne radiation is a significant concern in a post-nuclear environment, as radioactive fallout can contaminate rivers, lakes, and oceans, posing risks to human health and ecosystems. Understanding the pathways through which radiation enters water sources, its impact, and how to mitigate these risks is crucial for ensuring access to safe water. This chapter examines the risks associated with waterborne radiation and provides strategies for detecting, managing, and purifying contaminated water.

How Radiation Contaminates Water

1. **Fallout Deposition**:
    - Radioactive particles released during a nuclear event settle on water surfaces as fallout. Rain can wash additional particles from the atmosphere into rivers, lakes, and oceans.
2. **Runoff**:
    - Fallout particles on land are carried into water sources by rain, snowmelt, or flooding, concentrating contamination in rivers and reservoirs.
3. **Groundwater Contamination**:
    - Radioactive isotopes can seep into the soil and contaminate underground water supplies, affecting wells and springs.
4. **Marine Ecosystems**:
    - Oceans may absorb fallout from both atmospheric deposition and contaminated rivers. Currents can disperse these particles over vast areas.

Types of Radioactive Isotopes in Water

1. **Iodine-131**:
    - Short-lived (half-life ~8 days) but highly hazardous, primarily affecting thyroid health.
    - Enters water through fallout and is absorbed quickly by plants and animals.
2. **Cesium-137**:
    - Long-lived (half-life ~30 years) and water-soluble, making it a persistent contaminant in aquatic environments.
    - Accumulates in fish and marine life, entering the food chain.
3. **Strontium-90**:
    - Mimics calcium and accumulates in bones; its half-life is approximately 29 years.
    - Contaminates water through soil leaching and runoff.
4. **Plutonium-239**:
    - Extremely hazardous with a half-life of 24,000 years, though less soluble in water. It may still pose risks through sediment contamination.

Risks of Waterborne Radiation

1. **Health Impacts**:
    - Ingesting contaminated water can lead to internal radiation exposure, affecting organs, tissues, and DNA.
    - Long-term risks include cancer, thyroid disorders, and developmental issues in children.
2. **Ecological Damage**:
    - Radiation disrupts aquatic ecosystems, harming plants, fish, and other organisms.
    - Bioaccumulation occurs as radioactive isotopes move up the food chain, increasing concentrations in predators and humans.
3. **Economic and Social Effects**:
    - Contaminated water sources impact agriculture, fisheries, and livelihoods, exacerbating post-nuclear hardships.

Detecting Radiation in Water

1. **Radiation Detectors**:
    - Use Geiger counters or radiation survey meters to measure gamma radiation in and around water sources. While useful, these tools may not detect isotopes emitting only alpha or beta radiation.
2. **Water Sampling Kits**:
    - Specialized kits can test for specific isotopes, such as iodine-131 or cesium-137, in water samples.
3. **Sediment Testing**:
    - Test sediment from the bottom of rivers, lakes, and reservoirs, as radioactive particles often settle there.
4. **Visual Indicators**:
    - Look for dead fish, discolored water, or algae blooms, which may suggest contamination, though they are not definitive signs of radiation.

Strategies for Managing Waterborne Radiation

1. **Avoiding Contaminated Sources**:
    - Prioritize water from sealed, uncontaminated supplies, such as bottled water or deep wells protected from fallout.
2. **Testing and Monitoring**:
    - Regularly test water sources for radiation levels, especially after rainfall or flooding events that may introduce new contaminants.
3. **Collecting Rainwater Safely**:
    - Use clean, covered containers to collect rainwater after fallout has subsided (typically 24-48 hours post-event).
    - Test and treat rainwater before use.
4. **Sealed Storage**:
    - Store water in covered, sealed containers to prevent exposure to fallout particles.

Purifying Contaminated Water

Purification methods vary in effectiveness depending on the type and concentration of contamination.

1. **Boiling:**
   - Kills biological contaminants but does not remove radioactive isotopes.

1. **Distillation:**
   - Removes most radioactive particles by separating water vapor from contaminants, but requires fuel and time.
2. **Filtration:**
   - Use high-quality filters with activated carbon or ion exchange resins to remove radioactive isotopes like cesium-137 and iodine-131.
   - Reverse osmosis systems are particularly effective for removing radioactive contaminants.
3. **Chemical Treatments:**
   - Add potassium iodide to protect the thyroid from iodine-131 exposure, though this does not purify the water.
   - Use specific chemicals, such as ferric chloride, to bind and remove radioactive particles.

Long-Term Solutions for Water Safety

1. **Protecting Wells and Aquifers:**
   - Construct or retrofit wells with secure seals to prevent contamination from surface runoff.
   - Test groundwater regularly to ensure safety.
2. **Sediment Management:**
   - Dredge and safely dispose of contaminated sediment in rivers and lakes to reduce radiation levels.
3. **Alternative Water Sources:**
   - Explore desalination or the use of natural filtration systems for ocean water in coastal areas.
4. **Community Collaboration:**
   - Work with local communities to establish water safety protocols and share resources like testing equipment and purification systems.

Living with Waterborne Radiation Risks

1. **Rationing Clean Water:**
   - Prioritize drinking and cooking over non-essential uses, such as washing clothes or cleaning.
2. **Monitoring Aquatic Food Sources:**
   - Test fish and seafood for radiation before consumption, especially in contaminated rivers or coastal regions.
3. **Staying Informed:**
   - Keep updated on radiation levels in local water sources through community networks or official channels.

Psychological Considerations

The fear of invisible threats like waterborne radiation can create significant stress. Educate yourself and your family about detection and purification methods to alleviate anxiety and foster confidence in your ability to manage risks.

Final Thoughts

Waterborne radiation is a daunting challenge in a post-nuclear world, but understanding its behavior, risks, and solutions can help you secure safe water for survival. With vigilance, proper tools, and effective purification methods, it's possible to navigate this invisible danger and ensure your family's health and safety. By addressing both immediate needs and long-term solutions, you can adapt and thrive even in the face of contamination.

DIY Radiation Shields: Crafting Your Own Protective Gear

Radiation shields and protective gear are essential tools for reducing exposure in a fallout-contaminated environment. While professional-grade equipment offers the best protection, it is often inaccessible during a crisis. Fortunately, you can craft effective DIY radiation shields and protective gear using commonly available materials. This chapter explores how radiation shields work, the materials you'll need, and practical methods for creating your own protective solutions.

How Radiation Shields Work

Radiation shields protect against three main types of ionizing radiation:

1. **Alpha Radiation**:
    - Easily blocked by materials like paper, clothing, or a thin layer of metal.
    - Dangerous only if inhaled, ingested, or absorbed through wounds.
2. **Beta Radiation**:
    - Requires denser materials, such as plastic, wood, or thick clothing, to shield effectively.
    - Can penetrate skin but is less dangerous than gamma radiation.
3. **Gamma Radiation**:
    - Highly penetrating and requires dense, heavy materials like lead, concrete, or thick layers of water for effective shielding.
    - The most challenging type to block with DIY methods.

Materials for DIY Radiation Shields

Different materials offer varying levels of protection based on their density and thickness:

1. **Lead**:
    - Extremely effective but heavy and difficult to work with. Use thin lead sheets if available.
2. **Concrete**:
    - Provides good shielding, especially in thick layers. Concrete blocks or pre-mixed concrete can be used for stationary shields.
3. **Sand and Earth**:
    - Readily available and effective for gamma radiation. Sandbags or soil-filled barriers are easy to construct.
4. **Metal Sheets**:
    - Aluminium, steel, or tin sheets are lightweight options for portable shields.
5. **Water**:
    - Dense and versatile, water absorbs radiation well. Store in thick containers or use as a barrier in transparent tanks.
6. **Plastic and Wood**:
    - Useful for blocking beta radiation. Use thick plywood or stacked layers of heavy plastic.
7. **Clothing and Fabric**:
    - Layers of thick clothing, tarps, or blankets can shield against alpha and beta radiation.

DIY Protective Gear

Protective gear helps reduce direct exposure to radioactive particles and prevents inhalation or ingestion.

1. Respirators and Masks

- **Materials**: Use an N95 mask or higher-grade respirator for the best filtration. If unavailable, make a mask using multiple layers of fabric, tightly woven cloth, or activated carbon filters.
- **DIY Steps**:
    1. Cut a sturdy fabric into a mask shape, ensuring it covers the nose and mouth completely.
    2. Insert a layer of activated carbon or HEPA filter material for added protection.
    3. Secure with elastic straps or ties.

2. Protective Clothing

- **Materials**: Use waterproof or plastic-coated materials, such as raincoats, garbage bags, or painter's coveralls.
- **DIY Steps**:
    1. Create a suit by cutting and sealing garbage bags or tarp material with duct tape.
    2. Reinforce seams and openings to prevent fallout particles from entering.
    3. Add gloves and boots made of rubber or plastic for full-body coverage.

3. Goggles and Eye Shields

- **Materials**: Use swimming goggles or create shields with clear plastic sheets.
- **DIY Steps**:
    1. Cut clear plastic into shapes that fit snugly over your eyes.
    2. Secure with elastic bands or adhesive tape.

4. Gloves and Boots

- **Materials**: Use rubber gloves, dishwashing gloves, or even double-layered plastic bags for hands. For boots, wrap plastic or heavy-duty garbage bags over your footwear.
- **DIY Steps**:
    1. Tape the edges of gloves and boots to your clothing to seal gaps.
    2. Reinforce with duct tape for durability.

Building Stationary Radiation Shields

Stationary shields are essential for protecting shelter spaces, food supplies, or workstations.

1. Sandbag Walls

- **Materials**: Sand, soil, gravel, or similar dense materials; sandbags or burlap sacks.
- **DIY Steps**:
    1. Fill sandbags with dense material and seal tightly.
    2. Stack bags to create a wall at least 3 feet thick for effective gamma radiation shielding.

3. Arrange in layers to minimize gaps.

2. Water Barriers

- **Materials**: Large water containers, barrels, or storage tanks.
- **DIY Steps**:
    1. Fill containers with water and place them around your shelter walls.
    2. Stack or line up containers to form a dense barrier.

3. Concrete Blocks

- **Materials**: Pre-cast concrete blocks or bags of ready-mix concrete.
- **DIY Steps**:
    1. Stack blocks or pour mixed concrete into molds to create walls or barriers.
    2. Ensure walls are at least 6-8 inches thick for gamma radiation protection.

4. Metal Shields

- **Materials**: Aluminum, steel, or tin sheets; metal scraps.
- **DIY Steps**:
    1. Layer sheets or scraps to increase density.
    2. Position metal shields between you and radiation sources.

Portable Radiation Shields

Portable shields provide flexibility when moving through contaminated areas.

1. **Plywood and Metal Panels**:
    - Combine thick plywood with metal sheets for a lightweight but effective shield.
    - Attach handles or straps for easy carrying.
2. **Shielded Backpacks**:
    - Line the back panel of a sturdy backpack with lead sheets or dense material.
    - Use it as a protective barrier when walking away from radiation sources.
3. **Umbrella Shields**:
    - Cover a sturdy umbrella with aluminum or plastic sheets to shield against falling particles.

Maintaining DIY Radiation Shields

1. **Inspect Regularly**:
    - Check for wear, cracks, or damage that could reduce effectiveness.
2. **Reinforce as Needed**:
    - Add layers to shields if radiation levels increase or materials degrade.
3. **Decontaminate**:
    - Clean shields and gear with soap and water to remove fallout particles after use.

Limitations of DIY Shields

1. **Material Constraints**:
    ◦ DIY shields may not block high levels of gamma radiation without sufficient thickness or density.
2. **Mobility**:
    ◦ Portable shields are less effective than stationary ones due to weight and material limitations.
3. **Incomplete Protection**:
    ◦ DIY gear reduces exposure but may not fully eliminate risks, particularly for prolonged exposure.

Final Thoughts

While professional-grade protective equipment and shelters offer the best defense, DIY radiation shields and gear can significantly reduce exposure when resources are limited. By using readily available materials and adapting them creatively, you can craft solutions to protect yourself and your family. In a world of uncertainty, these shields offer a critical layer of safety, empowering you to face radiation risks with greater confidence.

Adapting Diets for Safety and Survival

Adapting your diet for safety and survival in a post-nuclear world is essential to maintain health and reduce the risks of consuming radioactive contaminants. Fallout can affect food supplies, making it necessary to carefully select, prepare, and grow food to minimize exposure to radiation. In this chapter, we'll explore practical strategies for modifying diets, ensuring proper nutrition, and preparing food safely in a contaminated environment.

Understanding Food Contamination

1. **How Fallout Affects Food**:
    - Fallout particles settle on the surfaces of crops, fruits, and vegetables.
    - Contaminated water used for irrigation or cooking introduces radioactive isotopes into food.
    - Livestock ingesting fallout-contaminated feed may pass isotopes into their milk, meat, or eggs.
2. **Key Isotopes of Concern**:
    - **Iodine-131**: Short-lived but harmful; concentrates in milk and leafy greens.
    - **Cesium-137**: Long-lived and accumulates in soft tissues, affecting meat and dairy.
    - **Strontium-90**: Mimics calcium, accumulating in bones and milk.

Prioritizing Safe Food Sources

1. **Stored Foods**:
    - Rely on pre-packaged, canned, or vacuum-sealed foods stored before the fallout. These are unlikely to be contaminated.
    - Wash the exterior of containers before opening to avoid transferring fallout particles.
2. **Clean Water**:
    - Ensure all water used for cooking or drinking is purified to avoid introducing radioactive particles into food.
3. **Indoor-Grown Produce**:
    - Grow vegetables and herbs in a controlled indoor environment using clean soil and water.
4. **Frozen Foods**:
    - Foods stored in freezers during the fallout may remain safe, but test and clean them thoroughly.

Nutritional Considerations in a Post-Nuclear Environment

1. **Caloric Needs**:
    - Prolonged stress, cold, and physical activity may increase caloric demands. Aim for high-calorie foods like nuts, seeds, and energy bars.
2. **Protein Sources**:
    - Canned meats, legumes, and powdered protein supplements can provide essential amino acids.
    - Avoid fresh meat from potentially contaminated animals unless it has been tested.
3. **Vitamins and Minerals**:
    - Limited access to fresh produce may lead to deficiencies. Include multivitamins or fortified foods to compensate.

1. **Fiber**:
   - ° Canned fruits, vegetables, and whole grains are important for digestion and overall health.

Food Preparation and Cooking for Safety

1. **Decontamination**:
   - ° Rinse produce with clean, running water and peel off outer layers to reduce surface contamination.
   - ° Soak foods like leafy greens in a solution of clean water and baking soda before rinsing.
2. **Cooking Techniques**:
   - ° Boiling, steaming, or roasting may help reduce surface contamination but does not remove radioactive isotopes absorbed internally.
   - ° Avoid frying or grilling foods that might concentrate contaminants in oils or fats.
3. **Storage**:
   - ° Keep food in sealed containers to prevent contamination from airborne particles.
   - ° Store perishables in cool, clean conditions to extend their shelf life.

Modifying Diets for Contaminated Environments

1. **Low-Absorption Foods**:
   - ° Focus on foods less likely to absorb radioactive isotopes, such as fruits with thick skins (bananas, oranges) and grains.
   - ° Avoid root vegetables like potatoes and carrots unless grown in clean soil.
2. **Alternative Proteins**:
   - ° Cultivate non-contaminated protein sources such as mushrooms, which can be grown indoors, or edible insects if culturally acceptable.
3. **Hydroponics and Aquaponics**:
   - ° Use these methods to grow clean produce and raise fish in controlled environments.
4. **Long-Term Preservation**:
   - ° Dry, can, or ferment foods to extend their usability while maintaining safety.

Rationing and Meal Planning

1. **Prioritize Nutrient-Dense Foods**:
   - ° Choose foods that provide maximum nutrition per calorie, such as beans, lentils, and fortified cereals.
2. **Plan for Sustainability**:
   - ° Rotate food supplies to ensure freshness and avoid waste.
   - ° Incorporate stored and fresh foods to create balanced meals.
3. **Emergency Rations**:
   - ° Reserve high-energy, long-lasting foods like energy bars or freeze-dried meals for periods of extreme need.

Growing Food Safely

1. **Indoor Gardening**:
    - Use clean containers, soil, and water to grow vegetables like lettuce, spinach, and herbs indoors.
    - Employ artificial lighting to ensure healthy plant growth.
2. **Soil Testing and Remediation**:
    - Test outdoor soil for radiation before planting.
    - Use raised beds filled with clean soil and line them with impermeable materials to prevent contamination.
3. **Crop Selection**:
    - Opt for fast-growing crops that spend less time absorbing contaminants.
    - Favor fruiting plants like tomatoes and peppers over root crops.

Psychological Benefits of Food

1. **Comfort Foods**:
    - Incorporate familiar and enjoyable foods to boost morale and provide a sense of normalcy.
2. **Cooking as a Ritual**:
    - Make meal preparation a communal activity to strengthen family bonds and reduce stress.
3. **Celebrations**:
    - Use food to mark milestones or achievements, reinforcing hope and resilience.

Long-Term Considerations

1. **Community Efforts**:
    - Share resources and knowledge with neighbors to establish safer, more sustainable food practices.
2. **Seed Saving**:
    - Preserve seeds from non-contaminated crops to ensure future planting opportunities.
3. **Monitoring and Testing**:
    - Regularly test food and water supplies for contamination to ensure ongoing safety.

Final Thoughts

Adapting your diet for safety and survival in a fallout-contaminated world is a balance between caution and creativity. By prioritizing clean food sources, modifying preparation methods, and focusing on nutritional needs, you can protect your health and sustain yourself in challenging conditions. Food is not only a necessity but also a source of comfort and connection—nurturing both body and spirit in times of adversity.

The Science of Mutation: What Radiation Does to Life

Radiation is a powerful force that can alter the very building blocks of life. Its ability to damage DNA and disrupt biological processes poses significant risks to all living organisms. Understanding the science of mutation caused by radiation helps us grasp its effects on humans, animals, and plants in a post-nuclear environment, and guides efforts to mitigate long-term impacts. This chapter delves into how radiation interacts with life at a molecular level, the types of mutations it causes, and the broader implications for survival and adaptation.

How Radiation Interacts with Living Organisms

Radiation affects living cells by damaging their DNA, the molecule that carries genetic instructions for growth, development, and reproduction. The type and severity of damage depend on the radiation dose, type, and duration of exposure.

1. **Ionizing Radiation**:
    - **Alpha Particles**: Cause significant damage to DNA when inhaled or ingested but are stopped by skin.
    - **Beta Particles**: Penetrate deeper into tissues, causing widespread damage.
    - **Gamma Rays and X-rays**: Highly penetrating and capable of damaging internal organs and deep tissues.
2. **Direct Effects**:
    - Radiation breaks the chemical bonds in DNA, leading to strand breaks and base damage.
    - Severe damage may result in cell death or malfunction.
3. **Indirect Effects**:
    - Radiation generates reactive oxygen species (ROS) in cells, which further damage DNA, proteins, and cell membranes.

Types of Radiation-Induced Mutations

Mutations are changes in the DNA sequence that occur when the cell fails to repair radiation damage correctly. These mutations can have various effects, ranging from harmless to lethal.

1. **Point Mutations**:
    - A single DNA base is altered, added, or removed. These subtle changes can disrupt genes, leading to diseases or malfunctioning proteins.
2. **Chromosomal Aberrations**:
    - Large-scale changes, such as deletions, duplications, inversions, or translocations of DNA segments. These mutations can cause cancer or developmental disorders.
3. **Genomic Instability**:
    - Radiation can trigger a cascade of genetic errors in future cell generations, increasing the likelihood of mutations over time.
4. **Cellular Outcomes**:
    - **Apoptosis**: Damaged cells self-destruct to prevent mutation spread.
    - **Carcinogenesis**: Cells with DNA mutations grow uncontrollably, leading to cancer.

- **Heritable Mutations**: Mutations in reproductive cells (sperm or eggs) can be passed to offspring, affecting future generations.

Effects of Radiation on Humans

1. **Short-Term Effects**:
   - High doses of radiation cause acute radiation syndrome (ARS), with symptoms like nausea, vomiting, hair loss, and immune suppression.
   - Localized exposure can lead to radiation burns or tissue necrosis.
2. **Long-Term Effects**:
   - Increased risk of cancers, especially leukemia and thyroid, breast, or lung cancers.
   - Genetic mutations passed to offspring, potentially causing developmental disorders or increased cancer susceptibility.
3. **Psychological Impact**:
   - Fear of mutation and illness can cause anxiety, depression, and social stigmatization.

Effects of Radiation on Animals

1. **Immediate Impact**:
   - High radiation doses kill cells in vital tissues, leading to organ failure or death.
   - Reproductive issues, such as reduced fertility or birth defects, arise from damaged germ cells.
2. **Ecological Changes**:
   - Sensitive species may die off, while more resilient organisms adapt or mutate.
   - Predators and prey dynamics may shift, disrupting ecosystems.
3. **Examples**:
   - Studies in Chernobyl have shown animals with malformed limbs, cataracts, and reduced life expectancy.

Effects of Radiation on Plants

1. **Growth and Development**:
   - Radiation can inhibit germination, stunt growth, and damage reproductive organs.
   - High doses may kill plants outright, while lower doses cause mutations that affect traits like color, shape, or yield.
2. **Adaptation and Mutation**:
   - Some plants develop resistance to radiation, while others exhibit mutated traits, such as altered leaf patterns or growth rates.
3. **Ecological Impact**:
   - Mutated plants may struggle to compete with more resilient species, altering biodiversity.

Mutation in Microorganisms

Microorganisms, including bacteria and fungi, are highly sensitive to radiation but can also adapt quickly due to their rapid reproduction rates.

1. **Beneficial Mutations:**
    - Some microorganisms evolve to thrive in radioactive environments, playing a role in breaking down radioactive waste or cycling nutrients in contaminated ecosystems.
2. **Risks:**
    - Mutations in pathogens may make them more virulent or resistant to treatments.

Evolutionary Implications

Radiation-induced mutations, while often harmful, can also drive evolutionary change. Over generations, species may adapt to contaminated environments through natural selection, with radiation-resistant traits becoming more common.

1. **Short-Term Adaptation:**
    - Organisms with advantageous mutations may survive and reproduce, altering the genetic makeup of populations.
2. **Long-Term Evolution:**
    - Persistent radiation exposure could lead to the emergence of entirely new traits or species better suited to high-radiation environments.

Mitigating Radiation's Effects on Life

1. **For Humans:**
    - Use shielding, decontamination, and protective clothing to minimize exposure.
    - Maintain a diet rich in antioxidants (e.g., vitamin C, E, selenium) to reduce DNA damage from reactive oxygen species.
2. **For Animals:**
    - Provide clean, uncontaminated feed and water.
    - Monitor wildlife for signs of radiation sickness or ecological imbalance.
3. **For Plants:**
    - Test and remediate soil before planting crops.
    - Grow plants in controlled, indoor environments when possible.

Psychological and Societal Considerations

Fear of mutation often leads to social stigma and discrimination against survivors of radiation exposure. Addressing these issues requires:

1. **Education:**
    - Provide accurate information about radiation effects and risks to reduce fear and misinformation.
2. **Support Systems:**
    - Establish community networks and counseling for those affected by radiation-related health issues.

3. **Scientific Research**:
    ◦ Continue studying radiation's effects to develop better protection and treatment methods.

Final Thoughts

Radiation's power to alter life at a molecular level is both a challenge and a testament to the resilience of living organisms. While mutations caused by radiation often result in harm, they also drive adaptation and evolution, underscoring life's capacity to endure. By understanding the science of mutation, we can better protect ourselves and our environment, while fostering hope for survival and recovery in a post-nuclear world.

The Importance of Hygiene in a Contaminated World

Hygiene becomes a cornerstone of survival in a contaminated world where radioactive fallout and other hazards infiltrate the environment. Maintaining cleanliness protects against radiation exposure, prevents the spread of illnesses, and promotes overall health and morale. This chapter explores the critical role of hygiene, strategies for staying clean in challenging conditions, and practical methods for safeguarding yourself and your family from invisible dangers.

Why Hygiene Matters in a Contaminated World

1. **Reducing Radiation Exposure**:
     - Fallout particles can cling to skin, hair, clothing, and surfaces, creating ongoing exposure risks.
     - Proper hygiene removes these particles, reducing both external and internal contamination.
2. **Preventing Illness**:
     - Weakened immune systems due to radiation exposure make individuals more susceptible to infections.
     - Poor hygiene can lead to the spread of bacteria, viruses, and parasites, compounding survival challenges.
3. **Psychological Benefits**:
     - Maintaining cleanliness fosters a sense of normalcy, control, and dignity, which are vital for mental well-being during crises.

Key Hygiene Challenges in a Post-Nuclear World

1. **Limited Water Supply**:
     - Clean water is scarce, requiring careful rationing and prioritization for hygiene and drinking.
2. **Contaminated Surfaces and Air**:
     - Fallout particles settle on every exposed surface, creating constant contamination risks.
3. **Inadequate Sanitation**:
     - Broken infrastructure often means no functioning toilets, showers, or waste disposal systems.
4. **Increased Waste**:
     - Handling waste safely becomes crucial to prevent disease and secondary contamination.

Personal Hygiene: Staying Clean in Contaminated Conditions

1. **Decontaminating Skin and Hair**:
     - Rinse exposed skin with clean water as soon as possible after suspected fallout exposure.
     - Use soap and lukewarm water to remove particles; avoid scrubbing to prevent abrasions that may allow radiation entry.
     - Wash hair without conditioner, as it can bind radioactive particles to the strands.
2. **Protecting Hands and Face**:
     - Wear gloves when handling contaminated materials and wash hands thoroughly after removal.
     - Use masks or scarves to cover your nose and mouth to prevent inhaling fallout particles.
3. **Clothing Care**:
     - Remove outer clothing before entering your shelter and seal it in plastic bags.

- ○ Wash contaminated clothing separately using clean water and detergent.

4. **Oral Hygiene:**
   - ○ Brush teeth regularly with clean water to prevent dental infections, even if resources are limited.
   - ○ Use baking soda or salt as an alternative to toothpaste if needed.

Managing Hygiene with Limited Water

1. **Dry Cleaning Methods:**
   - ○ Use wet wipes, alcohol-based hand sanitizers, or cloths moistened with a small amount of clean water.
   - ○ Focus on critical areas like hands, face, armpits, and groin.
2. **Prioritize Hygiene Needs:**
   - ○ Allocate water for drinking and essential hygiene first. Decontaminating fallout-exposed skin takes precedence over routine washing.
3. **Improvised Showers:**
   - ○ Use a spray bottle or container with a small opening to rinse areas of the body with minimal water usage.

Environmental Hygiene: Keeping Your Shelter Clean

1. **Regular Cleaning:**
   - ○ Wipe surfaces frequently with damp cloths to capture fallout particles.
   - ○ Use sealed plastic or cloth barriers over furniture and high-contact areas to simplify cleaning.
2. **Ventilation:**
   - ○ Use HEPA filters or improvised systems with dense fabric to filter air entering your shelter.
   - ○ Limit airflow from contaminated areas to reduce the spread of particles.
3. **Waste Management:**
   - ○ Store waste in sealed containers to prevent contamination and odor.
   - ○ Designate a specific area away from your living space for waste disposal if outdoors is accessible.

Sanitation: Managing Toileting and Waste

1. **Improvised Toilets:**
   - ○ Use buckets lined with heavy-duty plastic bags as makeshift toilets.
   - ○ Add absorbent materials like sawdust, sand, or ash to minimize odor and facilitate disposal.
2. **Human Waste Disposal:**
   - ○ Seal waste bags tightly and store them in a safe area until disposal is possible.
   - ○ Bury waste in deep, covered pits away from water sources if outdoor access is safe.
3. **Feminine Hygiene:**
   - ○ Stockpile reusable items like cloth pads or menstrual cups, which can be cleaned with minimal water.

Hygiene for Food and Water

1. **Cleaning Utensils:**
   - Wash dishes, pots, and utensils with clean water and detergent; rinse thoroughly.
   - Use disposable utensils or single-use liners for plates when water is scarce.
2. **Food Decontamination:**
   - Peel and rinse fruits and vegetables to remove fallout particles.
   - Avoid consuming food exposed to fallout unless tested and deemed safe.
3. **Water Purification:**
   - Boil, filter, or chemically treat water before use for drinking or washing.

Special Considerations for Children and the Elderly

1. **Children:**
   - Assist children with hygiene tasks to ensure thorough cleaning.
   - Use gentle, child-safe products to avoid skin irritation.
2. **Elderly:**
   - Provide extra support for those with mobility or cognitive challenges.
   - Focus on maintaining comfort and dignity while ensuring cleanliness.

Psychological Benefits of Hygiene

1. **Ritual and Routine:**
   - Establish regular hygiene practices to create a sense of structure and normalcy.
   - Involve the entire family in maintaining a clean environment to foster teamwork and morale.
2. **Focus on Small Wins:**
   - Celebrate simple achievements, like a clean living space or a refreshing wash, to boost spirits.

Long-Term Hygiene Planning

1. **Stockpiling Supplies:**
   - Store soap, hand sanitizers, disposable wipes, and absorbent materials.
   - Include large quantities of plastic bags for waste containment.
2. **Creating Clean Zones:**
   - Designate areas for specific activities (e.g., eating, sleeping, cleaning) to prevent cross-contamination.
3. **Improvisation Skills:**
   - Learn to use everyday items creatively for hygiene, such as making cleaning solutions from vinegar or baking soda.

Final Thoughts

Hygiene is often overlooked in survival planning, yet it is essential for health, safety, and emotional well-being in a contaminated world. By prioritizing cleanliness, using resources efficiently, and adapting to challenges, you can protect yourself and your loved ones from illness and radiation exposure. In the face of adversity, maintaining hygiene is not just about survival—it is a powerful act of resilience and self-care.

Creating a Fallout-Proof Wardrobe: Clothing for Safety

Creating a fallout-proof wardrobe is an essential step in preparing for survival in a post-nuclear environment. Proper clothing can act as a barrier against radioactive fallout particles, reducing exposure and contamination. The right materials, layering techniques, and maintenance practices can significantly enhance safety when venturing into or living in a contaminated world. This chapter explores how to build, use, and maintain a wardrobe designed for maximum protection.

The Role of Clothing in Radiation Protection

1. **Physical Barrier**:
   - Clothing prevents radioactive particles from coming into direct contact with the skin, reducing the risk of burns and contamination.
2. **Ease of Decontamination**:
   - Protective clothing allows you to remove outer layers that may have collected fallout particles, minimizing further exposure.
3. **Supplemental Shielding**:
   - While clothing cannot block gamma radiation, dense and layered materials provide partial shielding against beta and alpha particles.

Choosing the Right Materials

The effectiveness of your fallout-proof wardrobe depends on the materials used:

1. **Dense Fabrics**:
   - Opt for tightly woven materials like denim, canvas, or leather to reduce particle penetration.
   - Heavier fabrics offer better protection but may limit mobility and comfort.
2. **Waterproof Layers**:
   - Incorporate waterproof or plastic-coated materials to prevent fallout particles from adhering to the fabric.
   - Raincoats, ponchos, or plastic suits are ideal for outer layers.
3. **Synthetic Fabrics**:
   - Nylon and polyester are durable, easy to clean, and resistant to absorbing particles.
   - Avoid porous fabrics like wool or fleece for outer layers, as they can trap particles.
4. **Disposable Options**:
   - Consider disposable coveralls or hazmat suits for one-time use in heavily contaminated areas.

Building a Fallout-Proof Wardrobe

1. **Head Protection**:
   - Use hats or hoods made from waterproof materials to shield hair and scalp.
   - Tight-fitting head coverings like balaclavas provide full coverage.
2. **Face and Eye Shields**:
   - Include respirators or masks to prevent inhalation of radioactive particles.
   - Use goggles or face shields to protect eyes from fallout.

3. **Upper Body**:
   - Wear long-sleeve shirts or jackets with elastic cuffs to seal gaps.
   - Layer with a waterproof outer jacket to prevent contamination.
4. **Lower Body**:
   - Use durable pants made from dense materials like denim or canvas.
   - Waterproof pants or overalls are ideal for additional protection.
5. **Footwear**:
   - Sturdy, closed-toe boots made from leather or rubber are best.
   - Use waterproof gaiters or plastic covers to shield shoes from contamination.
6. **Gloves**:
   - Wear rubber or latex gloves as a base layer, with durable work gloves over them.
   - Ensure gloves fit snugly to prevent gaps.
7. **Outer Layer**:
   - The outermost layer should be waterproof and easy to clean or dispose of.
   - Use duct tape to seal seams and openings for a secure barrier.

Layering for Maximum Protection

1. **Base Layer**:
   - Wear lightweight, moisture-wicking fabrics to keep skin dry and comfortable.
   - Synthetic base layers like polyester or nylon are ideal.
2. **Mid Layer**:
   - Add insulating materials for warmth in cold conditions, such as fleece or synthetic blends.
   - Ensure mid-layers do not trap fallout particles.
3. **Outer Layer**:
   - Prioritize impermeable materials to block particles and protect underlying layers.
   - Seal all openings, including wrists, ankles, and necklines, with tape or elastic bands.

Maintaining and Decontaminating Clothing

1. **Decontamination**:
   - Remove outer layers carefully to avoid shaking or spreading particles.
   - Rinse clothing with clean water before removing it if possible.
   - Wash contaminated clothing separately using detergent and clean water.
2. **Storage**:
   - Store unused protective clothing in sealed, airtight containers to prevent exposure.
   - Use plastic bags or bins for easy access and organization.
3. **Inspection**:
   - Check clothing regularly for tears, holes, or wear that could compromise protection.
   - Repair damage immediately or replace items if repair is not possible.

DIY Fallout-Proof Clothing

If professional protective gear is unavailable, you can create your own:

1. **Plastic Suits**:
    - Use garbage bags or plastic sheeting to fashion improvised suits.
    - Seal with duct tape to prevent gaps.
2. **Homemade Masks**:
    - Layer fabric and activated carbon filters to create a DIY respirator.
    - Use tightly woven cotton or synthetic fabrics for the outer layers.
3. **Improvised Gloves**:
    - Double-layer plastic bags over hands and secure with tape.
4. **Rain Gear**:
    - Repurpose raincoats, ponchos, or tarps as protective outer layers.

Special Considerations for Children and the Elderly

1. **Children**:
    - Use lightweight, flexible materials to ensure mobility and comfort.
    - Adjust clothing sizes for a snug fit, sealing gaps around wrists, ankles, and necks.
2. **Elderly**:
    - Prioritize easy-to-don clothing with minimal fasteners or closures.
    - Ensure clothing allows for mobility aids like canes or walkers.

Psychological and Practical Benefits of a Fallout-Proof Wardrobe

1. **Peace of Mind**:
    - Knowing you have the right gear boosts confidence and reduces anxiety about exposure.
2. **Increased Mobility**:
    - Proper clothing allows you to safely perform outdoor tasks like gathering supplies or checking on livestock.
3. **Adaptability**:
    - A versatile wardrobe can be adjusted for different levels of contamination or weather conditions.

Long-Term Planning

1. **Stockpiling**:
    - Build a wardrobe with multiple sets of protective clothing for each family member.
    - Include items in a variety of sizes and materials for different conditions.
2. **Community Sharing**:
    - Coordinate with neighbors to pool resources and share surplus protective gear.
3. **Training and Drills**:
    - Practice donning and doffing protective clothing to ensure quick and effective use during emergencies.

Final Thoughts

A fallout-proof wardrobe is more than just clothing—it's a vital layer of defense against radioactive contamination. By carefully selecting materials, using proper layering techniques, and maintaining your gear, you can reduce exposure risks and confidently navigate a contaminated environment. With preparation and ingenuity, you can transform everyday items into life-saving protective gear, ensuring safety and resilience for you and your family.

Long-Term Shelter: Reinforcing and Upgrading Your Safe Haven

Establishing and maintaining a long-term shelter in a post-nuclear world is essential for surviving the prolonged hazards of radiation, environmental instability, and resource scarcity. While initial shelters focus on immediate safety, upgrading and reinforcing your safe haven ensures durability, comfort, and self-sufficiency over months or years. This chapter explores practical strategies for improving your shelter, from radiation protection and structural reinforcement to energy independence and psychological well-being.

Assessing Your Shelter's Current State

Before planning upgrades, evaluate your shelter's strengths and weaknesses:

1. **Radiation Protection**:
    - Assess existing barriers against gamma radiation, such as walls, ceilings, and floors.
    - Test radiation levels inside and around the shelter using a Geiger counter.
2. **Structural Integrity**:
    - Check for vulnerabilities like cracks, leaks, or weak support structures.
    - Evaluate the shelter's ability to withstand natural disasters, such as earthquakes or flooding.
3. **Resource Management**:
    - Determine the adequacy of your water, food storage, and waste disposal systems.
    - Identify areas where resource conservation or expansion is necessary.
4. **Comfort and Functionality**:
    - Assess ventilation, lighting, and space allocation to ensure long-term livability.

Reinforcing Radiation Shielding

1. **Thickening Walls**:
    - Add layers of concrete, brick, or packed earth to existing walls.
    - Use sandbags or lead sheets for portable or temporary shielding.
2. **Floor and Ceiling Protection**:
    - Install additional layers of shielding materials beneath floors and above ceilings.
    - Use dense materials like concrete or metal sheets.
3. **Window and Door Sealing**:
    - Replace windows with thick, leaded glass or cover them with removable shields.
    - Reinforce doors with metal or additional wooden layers, and use weatherstripping to seal gaps.
4. **Secondary Safe Room**:
    - Create an internal "safe zone" with maximum shielding for times of heightened radiation exposure.

Structural Reinforcement for Longevity

1. **Strengthening Foundations**:
    - Repair cracks in the foundation and add reinforcements like rebar or additional concrete layers.
    - Elevate the shelter if flooding is a concern.
2. **Weatherproofing**:
    - Seal leaks and insulate walls to protect against extreme temperatures and moisture.

- ◦ Use tarps, plastic sheeting, or waterproof coatings for temporary fixes.
3. **Reinforcing Roofs**:
    - ◦ Add support beams to roofs, especially if they must bear the weight of additional shielding.
    - ◦ Ensure proper drainage systems to prevent water pooling.
4. **Ventilation Upgrades**:
    - ◦ Install HEPA filters or create improvised air filtration systems to keep contaminated air out.
    - ◦ Build a manual ventilation system to maintain airflow in case of power outages.

Expanding Resources for Self-Sufficiency

1. **Water Supply**:
    - ◦ Increase water storage capacity with additional tanks or barrels.
    - ◦ Set up rainwater collection systems with filtration for long-term use.
2. **Food Production**:
    - ◦ Incorporate indoor gardening systems like hydroponics or container gardening.
    - ◦ Allocate space for growing herbs, vegetables, or microgreens under artificial light.
3. **Energy Independence**:
    - ◦ Install solar panels or small wind turbines for renewable energy.
    - ◦ Use hand-crank or pedal-powered generators for emergency power.
4. **Waste Management**:
    - ◦ Build composting systems for organic waste.
    - ◦ Designate an area for safely storing and disposing of non-biodegradable waste.

Enhancing Comfort and Liveability

1. **Lighting**:
    - ◦ Use energy-efficient LED lights powered by solar panels or batteries.
    - ◦ Reflective surfaces can maximize light distribution.
2. **Space Optimization**:
    - ◦ Organize storage with shelves, bins, and vertical space-saving solutions.
    - ◦ Create multi-purpose areas, such as folding beds or retractable tables.
3. **Heating and Cooling**:
    - ◦ Install insulation to regulate indoor temperatures.
    - ◦ Use compact, fuel-efficient heaters and fans to manage temperature extremes.
4. **Psychological Well-Being**:
    - ◦ Decorate with personal items, artwork, or plants to create a sense of normalcy.
    - ◦ Designate areas for relaxation, exercise, and communal activities.

Security Measures

1. **Fortifying Entrances**:
    - ◦ Install heavy-duty locks, reinforced doors, and bars or shutters on windows.
    - ◦ Build barriers or trenches around the shelter to deter unauthorized access.
2. **Surveillance**:
    - ◦ Set up low-tech alarm systems like tripwires or bells to monitor the perimeter.

◦ Use battery-powered cameras or motion sensors for advanced security.

3. **Escape Routes:**
    - ◦ Plan and prepare alternative exits in case the main entrance is compromised.
    - ◦ Ensure escape routes are shielded and accessible.

Preparing for Long-Term Maintenance

1. **Repair Supplies:**
    - ◦ Stock tools, spare parts, and materials for ongoing maintenance.
    - ◦ Learn basic repair skills for plumbing, electrical systems, and structural fixes.
2. **Pest Control:**
    - ◦ Seal entry points and store food in airtight containers to prevent infestations.
    - ◦ Use natural repellents or traps to manage pests without introducing toxins.
3. **Routine Inspections:**
    - ◦ Regularly inspect for structural issues, radiation leaks, or resource shortages.
    - ◦ Create a checklist to track maintenance tasks.

Training and Community Collaboration

1. **Skill Development:**
    - ◦ Teach family members survival skills like water purification, food preservation, and basic first aid.
    - ◦ Rotate responsibilities to ensure everyone can manage essential tasks.
2. **Community Networks:**
    - ◦ Collaborate with neighbors or nearby groups to share resources and expertise.
    - ◦ Establish communication systems, such as radios, for coordination.

Psychological Resilience in Long-Term Shelters

1. **Create Routines:**
    - ◦ Establish daily schedules for tasks, meals, and downtime to provide structure.
2. **Encourage Creativity:**
    - ◦ Include hobbies or activities that foster creativity, such as drawing, writing, or crafting.
3. **Foster Connection:**
    - ◦ Spend time together as a family or group to maintain strong emotional bonds.

Final Thoughts

A long-term shelter is more than a protective space—it's a foundation for survival, comfort, and resilience. By reinforcing and upgrading your safe haven, you can adapt to evolving challenges and create an environment that sustains both physical and mental well-being. Preparedness, ingenuity, and ongoing effort transform a basic shelter into a true sanctuary for navigating a post-nuclear world.

Understanding Radiation Decay: How Time Changes the Danger

Radiation decay is a critical concept for understanding how the dangers of nuclear fallout diminish over time. Radioactive materials emit ionizing radiation as they decay into more stable forms, a process that occurs at predictable rates depending on the isotopes involved. By understanding the principles of radiation decay, you can make informed decisions about when it is safer to venture outside, use resources, or return to contaminated areas. This chapter explores the science of radiation decay, how time reduces exposure risks, and practical strategies for navigating a fallout-contaminated world.

What Is Radiation Decay?

Radiation decay, or radioactive decay, is the process by which unstable atomic nuclei lose energy by emitting radiation. This radiation can take the form of:

1. **Alpha Particles**:
   - Large and heavy; blocked by skin or clothing but dangerous if inhaled or ingested.
2. **Beta Particles**:
   - Smaller and more penetrating; can damage skin and internal tissues.
3. **Gamma Rays**:
   - Highly penetrating and capable of passing through thick materials, posing the greatest external hazard.

Each radioactive isotope has a unique decay rate, measured by its **half-life**—the time it takes for half of the radioactive material to decay.

The Rule of Sevens and Radiation Decay

In a nuclear fallout scenario, radiation levels decrease rapidly in the first few days due to the decay of short-lived isotopes. This pattern is summarized by the **"Rule of Sevens"**:

1. **First 7 Hours**:
   - Radiation levels drop to about 10% of their initial intensity.
2. **First 48 Hours (2 Days)**:
   - Radiation decreases further to approximately 1% of the initial level.
3. **First 14 Days (2 Weeks)**:
   - Radiation falls to 0.1% of the original intensity, making most areas significantly safer.

These rapid reductions are primarily due to the decay of isotopes with short half-lives, such as iodine-131.

Key Radioactive Isotopes and Their Half-Lives

Understanding the isotopes present in fallout helps assess long-term risks:

1. **Iodine-131**:
   - Half-life: ~8 days.
   - Primary concern in the first weeks due to its impact on the thyroid.

2. **Cesium-137**:
   - Half-life: ~30 years.
   - Long-term contaminant that accumulates in soil, plants, and animals.
3. **Strontium-90**:
   - Half-life: ~29 years.
   - Mimics calcium, accumulating in bones and posing long-term health risks.
4. **Plutonium-239**:
   - Half-life: ~24,000 years.
   - Extremely toxic but less mobile in the environment.

Practical Implications of Radiation Decay

1. **Immediate Safety**:
   - Shelter in place for at least the first 48 hours when radiation levels are highest.
   - Use this time to monitor radiation levels inside and outside your shelter with detection tools.
2. **Short-Term Recovery**:
   - After two weeks, many areas may be safe for limited outdoor activity, depending on fallout density and geographic factors.
   - Continue wearing protective gear and limit time outside.
3. **Long-Term Risks**:
   - Isotopes like cesium-137 and strontium-90 remain hazardous for decades, especially in soil and food supplies.
   - Regular testing of the environment and food sources is essential.

Radiation Decay in the Environment

1. **Airborne Radiation**:
   - Fallout particles settle within hours to days, significantly reducing airborne risks.
   - Use HEPA filters and ventilated spaces to maintain clean indoor air.
2. **Soil Contamination**:
   - Radioactive isotopes bind to soil particles, with levels decreasing slowly over years or decades.
   - Remediate soil with techniques like removal, sealing, or phytoremediation.
3. **Water Sources**:
   - Contaminated water may remain hazardous as isotopes like cesium-137 dissolve and persist.
   - Test and purify water before use.

Monitoring Radiation Over Time

1. **Geiger Counters**:
   - Measure overall radiation levels to assess immediate dangers.
   - Use frequently in the first few days post-fallout.
2. **Dosimeters**:
   - Track cumulative radiation exposure over time to ensure safe limits are not exceeded.
3. **Regular Testing**:
   - Conduct periodic tests of air, soil, water, and food to monitor changes in contamination levels.

Strategies for Living with Radiation Decay

1. **Sheltering and Shielding**:
    - Maintain shielding measures for the first two weeks when radiation levels are highest.
    - Gradually reduce reliance on shelter as levels drop but remain cautious in high-risk areas.
2. **Time and Distance**:
    - Minimize time spent in contaminated areas and maximize distance from radiation sources.
3. **Decontamination**:
    - Regularly clean surfaces, clothing, and skin to reduce secondary exposure.
4. **Adaptation**:
    - Shift activities to safer areas and times as radiation levels decline.
    - Develop long-term solutions, such as indoor farming or controlled water systems, for contaminated resources.

Psychological Considerations

Understanding radiation decay helps reduce fear and uncertainty. By tracking radiation levels and observing predictable declines, you can make rational, informed decisions about safety and recovery. This knowledge fosters a sense of control and empowers communities to adapt over time.

Looking to the Future

As time passes, the decreasing intensity of radiation allows for gradual recovery and rebuilding. Long-term planning includes:

1. **Environmental Remediation**:
    - Implement strategies to clean contaminated land and water sources.
2. **Community Resettlement**:
    - Monitor and identify areas safe for habitation as radiation levels fall.
3. **Sustainable Living**:
    - Adapt to the lingering presence of long-lived isotopes with innovative techniques for agriculture and resource management.

Final Thoughts

Radiation decay transforms the initial chaos of a nuclear fallout event into a manageable reality over time. By understanding how isotopes decay and how danger diminishes, you can make informed decisions that protect your health and enable recovery. Knowledge of radiation decay is not just a survival tool—it's a foundation for hope and resilience in the face of adversity.

Protecting Your Eyes and Skin: Combatting UV and Radiation Damage

Protecting your eyes and skin from UV and radiation damage in a post-nuclear world is vital for survival and maintaining long-term health. Increased UV exposure due to ozone layer depletion and the direct effects of ionizing radiation from fallout pose significant risks. This chapter focuses on understanding these dangers, how they impact your body, and practical strategies to protect yourself effectively.

The Dual Threat: UV and Ionizing Radiation

1. **UV Radiation:**
   - Caused by sunlight, UV radiation can increase due to nuclear explosions that damage the ozone layer.
   - Risks include sunburn, premature aging, skin cancer, and cataracts.
2. **Ionizing Radiation:**
   - Released by fallout, ionizing radiation can penetrate skin and tissue, causing burns, DNA damage, and long-term health risks like cancer.

Both types of radiation can act independently or synergistically, amplifying harm in exposed environments.

Effects of Radiation on Skin and Eyes

Skin

1. **Sunburn and Radiation Burns:**
   - UV radiation causes superficial burns, while ionizing radiation can penetrate deeper, damaging cells and tissues.
   - Radiation burns often appear hours or days after exposure, with symptoms like redness, blistering, or peeling.
2. **Chronic Damage:**
   - Prolonged UV exposure leads to premature aging, loss of skin elasticity, and increased skin cancer risk.
   - Long-term exposure to fallout radiation can cause chronic skin conditions or delayed cancers.
3. **Infection Risks:**
   - Skin weakened by burns or irritation becomes vulnerable to bacterial or fungal infections.

Eyes

1. **Photokeratitis (Snow Blindness):**
   - UV exposure causes painful inflammation of the cornea, leading to temporary vision loss.
2. **Cataracts:**
   - Both UV and ionizing radiation can damage the lens of the eye, causing cloudiness and vision impairment over time.
3. **Retinal Damage:**
   - Ionizing radiation may damage retinal cells, potentially leading to permanent vision loss.

Immediate Protection Measures

Skin

1. **Clothing**:
   - Wear long-sleeve shirts and pants made of tightly woven, lightweight fabric to shield skin from UV and fallout.
   - Use waterproof or plastic-coated outer layers to prevent fallout particles from adhering.
2. **Lotions and Sunscreen**:
   - Apply broad-spectrum sunscreen with SPF 30 or higher to exposed areas. Reapply every two hours or after sweating.
   - Look for sunscreens with zinc oxide or titanium dioxide for maximum protection.
3. **Barrier Methods**:
   - Use gloves, hats, and scarves to cover vulnerable areas like hands, neck, and face.
4. **Shelter**:
   - Stay indoors during peak sunlight hours or immediately after fallout events when radiation levels are highest.

Eyes

1. **Sunglasses**:
   - Wear UV-blocking sunglasses that protect against both UVA and UVB rays.
   - Wraparound styles provide additional protection from peripheral light.
2. **Eye Shields**:
   - Use clear safety goggles to protect against fallout particles and windborne debris.
3. **Rest and Avoidance**:
   - Limit direct exposure to sunlight or contaminated environments.

Long-Term Protection Strategies

1. **Protective Clothing**:
   - Invest in UV-resistant fabrics or layer clothing to enhance protection.
   - Maintain a dedicated set of clean, decontaminated clothing for outdoor activities.
2. **Moisturizers and Healing Creams**:
   - Use products containing aloe vera, vitamin E, or hyaluronic acid to soothe and repair sun or radiation-damaged skin.
3. **Hydration**:
   - Keep skin healthy and resilient by drinking plenty of water and avoiding dehydration.
4. **Diet for Skin Health**:
   - Consume foods rich in antioxidants, such as berries, leafy greens, and nuts, to combat free radical damage from radiation.
   - Include vitamin C and E supplements to support skin repair and immunity.
5. **Protecting Children and Elderly**:
   - Children's thinner skin and elderly individuals' compromised tissue repair make them especially vulnerable. Use extra precautions to ensure they are adequately covered and hydrated.

Mitigating Fallout and UV Risks in the Environment

1. **Creating Shaded Areas**:
    - Use tarps, reflective sheets, or improvised barriers to reduce direct sunlight exposure near shelters.
2. **Building UV and Fallout Shields**:
    - Install protective window films or use heavy curtains to block UV and gamma rays indoors.
3. **Decontamination Protocols**:
    - Wash skin and clothing thoroughly after exposure to fallout to prevent secondary contamination.
    - Rinse eyes with clean water if irritation occurs.

Treating Damage from UV and Radiation Exposure

1. **Skin**:
    - For mild sunburn: Apply cool compresses, aloe vera gel, or over-the-counter hydrocortisone cream to reduce inflammation.
    - For radiation burns: Rinse with clean water, cover with sterile dressings, and monitor for infection. Seek medical attention if blisters or open wounds develop.
2. **Eyes**:
    - For photokeratitis: Rest in a dark environment, apply cool compresses, and use lubricating eye drops to alleviate discomfort.
    - For cataracts or vision loss: Monitor symptoms and seek professional evaluation if surgery becomes available.

Psychological and Practical Benefits of Protection

1. **Confidence and Control**:
    - Knowing you have the tools to protect yourself reduces anxiety and allows for safer outdoor activities.
2. **Prevention of Long-Term Issues**:
    - Proactively guarding against UV and fallout damage prevents chronic health problems, enhancing quality of life.

Planning for Future Protection

1. **Stockpiling Essentials**:
    - Keep a supply of sunscreen, sunglasses, protective clothing, and first-aid materials for treating burns and irritation.
2. **Education and Practice**:
    - Teach family members about the importance of UV and fallout protection.
    - Practice using protective gear and decontamination protocols.
3. **Monitoring Conditions**:
    - Regularly test environmental radiation levels and UV index to plan safe outdoor activities.

Final Thoughts

Protecting your eyes and skin is not just about survival—it's about preserving your ability to thrive and maintain health in a challenging environment. By understanding the risks and implementing effective protective measures, you can reduce exposure, minimize damage, and adapt to life in a world where both UV and ionizing radiation are constant threats. Empowered by preparation and knowledge, you ensure a safer and healthier future for yourself and your loved ones.

How to Recognize and Avoid Secondary Threats

In a post-nuclear world, secondary threats—those arising as a consequence of the initial disaster—pose significant dangers to survivors. These threats include disease outbreaks, contaminated resources, psychological strain, and societal instability. Recognizing and mitigating these risks is essential for long-term survival. This chapter explores how to identify secondary threats, understand their origins, and implement strategies to protect yourself and your community.

What Are Secondary Threats?

Secondary threats are hazards indirectly caused by the primary nuclear event. These dangers arise as fallout disrupts natural systems, infrastructure, and social order, creating cascading challenges.

1. **Environmental**:
    - Contaminated air, water, soil, and food.
    - Spread of radioactive particles through wind, rain, and erosion.
2. **Biological**:
    - Disease outbreaks due to poor sanitation, weakened immune systems, and overcrowding.
    - Vector-borne illnesses as insects and animals adapt to new conditions.
3. **Social**:
    - Breakdown of law and order, leading to looting, violence, and exploitation.
    - Misinformation and panic spreading within communities.
4. **Psychological**:
    - Trauma, anxiety, and depression impacting decision-making and relationships.
    - Long-term effects of isolation and fear.

Recognizing Secondary Threats

Environmental Threats

1. **Signs of Contaminated Resources**:
    - Water: Discoloration, unusual odors, or dead aquatic life.
    - Food: Mold, spoilage, or crops grown in untested soil.
    - Air: Presence of ash, soot, or increased radiation readings.
2. **Indicators of Fallout Spread**:
    - Changes in weather patterns, such as fallout-laden rain or snow.
    - High radiation levels detected in previously safe areas.

Biological Threats

1. **Disease Outbreaks**:
    - Symptoms like fever, vomiting, diarrhea, and skin rashes in multiple individuals.
    - Increased insect activity, such as mosquitoes or flies, near waste or water.
2. **Animal Behavior**:
    - Unusual behavior in wildlife due to contamination or habitat disruption.
    - Increased presence of pests, such as rodents, in shelters or food stores.

Social Threats

1. **Civil Unrest:**
   - Groups or individuals attempting to seize resources.
   - Escalating violence or theft in nearby areas.
2. **Exploitation:**
   - False promises of safety or aid in exchange for goods or compliance.
   - Scams or coercion targeting vulnerable survivors.

Psychological Threats

1. **Mental Health Signs:**
   - Withdrawal, irritability, or paranoia in yourself or others.
   - Difficulty concentrating or making decisions.
2. **Group Dynamics:**
   - Increased conflict or breakdown of trust within families or communities.

Strategies for Avoiding Secondary Threats

Environmental Threats

1. **Test and Monitor:**
   - Regularly test air, water, and soil for contamination using appropriate tools.
   - Establish a schedule for testing to catch changes early.
2. **Control Exposure:**
   - Limit time spent in outdoor areas with high contamination risks.
   - Use protective gear when handling potentially contaminated resources.
3. **Secure Resources:**
   - Store food and water in sealed, uncontaminated containers.
   - Avoid consuming crops or livestock without thorough testing.

Biological Threats

1. **Hygiene:**
   - Maintain personal and environmental cleanliness to prevent disease.
   - Wash hands, decontaminate surfaces, and dispose of waste properly.
2. **Sanitation:**
   - Use makeshift toilets with sealed bags or containers.
   - Treat waste with lime, ash, or chemicals to neutralize pathogens.
3. **Pest Control:**
   - Seal shelters to prevent entry by insects or rodents.
   - Use traps, repellents, or natural deterrents to manage pests.
4. **Medical Preparedness:**
   - Stockpile basic medications, antibiotics, and first-aid supplies.
   - Isolate sick individuals to prevent the spread of illness.

Social Threats

1. **Situational Awareness**:
   - Stay informed about local events through radios or trusted networks.
   - Observe surroundings for signs of unrest or opportunistic individuals.
2. **Community Collaboration**:
   - Build alliances with trusted neighbors or groups for mutual protection.
   - Share resources strategically to avoid drawing unwanted attention.
3. **Defensive Measures**:
   - Secure your shelter with reinforced doors, windows, and simple alarm systems.
   - Develop an escape plan in case of intrusions or danger.

Psychological Threats

1. **Mental Health Support**:
   - Engage in regular communication with family or community members.
   - Practice mindfulness, journaling, or other stress-relief techniques.
2. **Structure and Routine**:
   - Establish daily schedules for tasks and rest to provide stability.
   - Include recreational activities to boost morale.
3. **Conflict Resolution**:
   - Address disputes calmly and fairly to maintain group cohesion.
   - Rotate responsibilities to prevent burnout and resentment.

Preparing for Long-Term Resilience

1. **Resource Stockpiling**:
   - Maintain reserves of clean water, food, and medical supplies.
   - Include tools for testing and purifying resources as contamination persists.
2. **Education and Skills Training**:
   - Learn basic first aid, waste management, and pest control techniques.
   - Teach family members survival skills to reduce reliance on external aid.
3. **Adaptability**:
   - Stay flexible in the face of changing conditions, from environmental shifts to societal challenges.

Recognizing Early Warning Signs

1. **Environmental Changes**:
   - Monitor radiation levels and environmental conditions regularly.
2. **Health Patterns**:
   - Track symptoms among family or group members to detect potential outbreaks.
3. **Social Climate**:
   - Pay attention to shifts in local behavior, such as increased desperation or aggression.

Final Thoughts

Secondary threats are inevitable in a post-nuclear environment, but they can be managed with vigilance, preparation, and adaptability. By recognizing early warning signs, maintaining hygiene and sanitation, and fostering a strong, cooperative community, you can mitigate these dangers and build a sustainable path forward. Protecting yourself from secondary threats is not just about survival—it's about creating a foundation for recovery and resilience in the face of ongoing challenges.

Clean Meat: Raising Radiation-Free Animals

Raising radiation-free animals for clean meat is a critical part of long-term survival and rebuilding food security in a post-nuclear world. Ensuring that livestock remains uncontaminated requires thoughtful planning, controlled environments, and a deep understanding of how radioactive fallout affects the food chain. This chapter explores how to raise healthy, safe animals, from protecting them against radiation exposure to managing their feed and water supplies.

Understanding the Impact of Radiation on Livestock

Radioactive fallout affects animals in similar ways to humans, with contamination occurring through inhalation, ingestion, or direct exposure. Fallout particles settle on grazing land, water sources, and feed, entering animals' bodies and accumulating in their tissues.

1. **Key Isotopes of Concern**:
    - **Iodine-131**: Accumulates in the thyroid gland, affecting milk production in dairy animals.
    - **Cesium-137**: Mimics potassium, concentrating in muscles (meat).
    - **Strontium-90**: Mimics calcium, accumulating in bones and milk.
2. **Health Effects on Animals**:
    - Acute radiation sickness at high doses, leading to illness or death.
    - Long-term issues like reduced fertility, weakened immune systems, and stunted growth.
3. **Risks to Humans**:
    - Consuming contaminated meat, milk, or eggs can lead to internal radiation exposure and health problems.

Protecting Livestock from Radiation

1. Sheltering Animals

- Build radiation-shielded enclosures with thick walls made of concrete, brick, or earth.
- Cover roofs with dense materials or additional layers of soil for gamma radiation protection.
- Seal gaps and openings to prevent fallout particles from entering.

2. Controlled Grazing

- Avoid letting animals graze on open fields where fallout may have settled.
- Use raised feeding systems, such as troughs, to keep feed away from contaminated soil.

3. Protective Barriers

- Cover animals with lightweight protective blankets or tarps during outdoor exposure.
- Limit their time outside and monitor radiation levels in grazing areas.

Ensuring Clean Feed and Water

1. Feed Management

- Stockpile clean, uncontaminated feed in sealed, airtight containers before fallout occurs.
- Grow fodder indoors using hydroponic or container systems with purified soil and water.
- Supplement diets with stored grains, hay, and commercially prepared animal feed tested for radiation.

2. Water Safety

- Provide livestock with clean, filtered water from uncontaminated sources, such as sealed rainwater tanks or deep wells.
- Regularly test water for radioactive particles and purify using distillation or ion exchange filters.

Selecting and Managing Livestock

Certain animals are better suited to controlled environments and provide versatile food sources. Choose species based on their adaptability, size, and resource needs.

1. Small Livestock

- **Chickens**: Produce eggs and meat, require less space, and adapt well to confined systems.
- **Rabbits**: Breed quickly, need minimal feed, and thrive in small enclosures.
- **Ducks and Geese**: Provide eggs and meat; can be raised in water-conserving systems.

2. Larger Livestock

- **Goats**: Versatile for milk and meat production, require less grazing space than cows.
- **Sheep**: Provide meat and wool; can adapt to penned environments.
- **Cattle**: Useful for milk and meat but require larger shelters and significant feed.

Monitoring and Testing for Contamination

1. **Radiation Detection Tools**:
   - Use Geiger counters or specialized detectors to test animal feed, water, and living areas regularly.
   - Monitor livestock themselves for signs of radiation sickness, such as lethargy, reduced appetite, or hair loss.
2. **Milk and Meat Testing**:
   - Test milk and meat for radioactive isotopes before consumption or sale.
   - Avoid products from animals grazing on untested land.
3. **Soil and Feed Testing**:
   - Test soil used for growing fodder and feed sources to ensure they are free of contamination.

Breeding and Herd Management

1. **Breeding in Controlled Environments**:
   ◦ Focus on breeding animals within protected areas to avoid exposing newborns to contamination.
   ◦ Rotate breeding pairs to maintain genetic diversity and healthy offspring.
2. **Isolating Sick Animals**:
   ◦ Remove animals showing symptoms of illness or contamination from the main herd.
   ◦ Treat minor injuries and illnesses promptly to prevent complications.
3. **Culling and Disposal**:
   ◦ Humanely cull heavily contaminated or sick animals to prevent further contamination.
   ◦ Dispose of carcasses safely, following decontamination protocols.

Building a Sustainable Livestock System

1. **Indoor Farming**:
   ◦ Create enclosed barns or shelters with controlled ventilation and climate systems.
   ◦ Use hydroponics or indoor farming for clean feed production.
2. **Waste Management**:
   ◦ Collect and compost animal waste in sealed systems to minimize contamination spread.
   ◦ Use waste as fertilizer only after testing for safety.
3. **Community Collaboration**:
   ◦ Share resources, expertise, and livestock with neighbors to build resilience and mutual support.
   ◦ Establish cooperative breeding programs to maintain healthy herds.

Long-Term Strategies for Clean Meat

1. **Rotational Grazing**:
   ◦ Use tested, clean areas for grazing in rotation to reduce contamination risk.
2. **Alternative Protein Sources**:
   ◦ Explore insect farming (e.g., crickets, mealworms) for sustainable, radiation-free protein.
3. **Monitoring Over Generations**:
   ◦ Track radiation levels in livestock across multiple generations to ensure genetic health and contamination reduction.

Psychological and Nutritional Benefits

1. **Food Security**:
   ◦ Raising livestock provides a reliable source of meat, milk, and eggs, reducing dependence on external resources.
2. **Morale Boost**:
   ◦ Caring for animals fosters a sense of purpose and normalcy, enhancing emotional well-being.
3. **Nutritional Value**:
   ◦ Clean meat supplies essential proteins, fats, and nutrients crucial for long-term survival and health.

Final Thoughts

Raising radiation-free animals is both a challenge and an opportunity in a post-nuclear world. By understanding the risks of fallout, implementing protective measures, and maintaining rigorous testing and monitoring, you can ensure safe and sustainable meat production. Livestock not only provide vital nourishment but also serve as a cornerstone for rebuilding a resilient and self-sufficient future.

Radioactive Zones: Maps and Indicators for Survival

Navigating and understanding radioactive zones is essential for survival in a post-nuclear world. Fallout does not distribute evenly, creating areas with varying levels of radiation. Identifying these zones and understanding their risks allows you to make informed decisions about travel, shelter, and resource use. This chapter explores how to interpret radioactive zones, create survival maps, and use indicators to avoid dangerous areas.

What Are Radioactive Zones?

Radioactive zones are areas contaminated by nuclear fallout, characterized by varying levels of ionizing radiation. These zones depend on factors such as:

Proximity to Blast Sites:

Areas near ground zero of nuclear explosions experience the highest radiation levels.

Explosions at higher altitudes (airbursts) may produce less localized fallout but distribute particles over a wider area.

Wind and Weather Patterns:

Wind direction and speed carry fallout particles, often creating long, narrow trails of contamination downwind from the blast site.

Rain or snow can concentrate fallout in specific locations, forming "hot spots."

Terrain and Geography:

Valleys and low-lying areas may trap fallout particles, while higher elevations may experience less accumulation.

Urban areas with dense structures may shield some locations while concentrating fallout in open spaces.

Radiation Levels and Zones of Contamination

Radioactive zones are generally categorized by their radiation intensity, measured in **roentgens per hour (R/h)** or **sieverts per hour (Sv/h)**:

Severe Contamination Zone:

Radiation Levels: >10 R/h or 0.1 Sv/h.

Characteristics: Immediate health risks, including radiation sickness and death with short exposure.

Safety: Avoid entirely; no safe duration for unprotected exposure.

High Contamination Zone:

Radiation Levels: 1-10 R/h or 0.01-0.1 Sv/h.

Characteristics: Dangerous for prolonged exposure; requires protective gear and limited time outdoors.

Safety: Use only for essential activities with maximum precautions.

Moderate Contamination Zone:

Radiation Levels: 0.1-1 R/h or 0.001-0.01 Sv/h.

Characteristics: Long-term exposure increases cancer risk but is manageable with precautions.

Safety: Suitable for short stays with protective measures.

Low Contamination Zone:

Radiation Levels: <0.1 R/h or 0.001 Sv/h.

Characteristics: Close to background radiation levels; relatively safe for habitation and farming.

Safety: Regular monitoring and periodic testing recommended.

Mapping Radioactive Zones

1. Interpreting Fallout Patterns

- Use prevailing wind maps and known blast locations to predict fallout paths.
- Identify high-risk areas downwind from explosions or close to water sources, as fallout spreads through rivers and lakes.

2. Creating Survival Maps

- **Gather Data**:
    - Use Geiger counters, dosimeters, or online resources to measure and record radiation levels in your area.
- **Mark Contaminated Areas**:
    - Highlight zones of severe, high, moderate, and low contamination based on radiation readings.
- **Include Landmarks**:
    - Note natural barriers (hills, rivers) and human structures (bridges, roads) that affect accessibility and fallout dispersion.
- **Update Regularly**:
    - Radiation levels decrease over time; revise maps periodically as areas become safer.

3. Utilizing Existing Resources

- Consult pre-existing fallout maps and government data for known contamination zones.
- Use weather apps or services to track wind patterns and rainfall, which affect fallout movement.

Indicators of Radioactive Zones

Natural Indicators

1. **Vegetation**:
    ◦ Wilting, discoloration, or absence of plant life may indicate high contamination.
    ◦ Stunted growth in crops or wild plants suggests long-term radiation exposure.
2. **Wildlife**:
    ◦ Dead or sick animals, especially in clusters, are a warning sign of dangerous radiation levels.
    ◦ Unusual animal behavior, such as lethargy or disorientation, may also indicate contamination.

Environmental Changes

1. **Water**:
    ◦ Discoloured or foul-smelling water, combined with dead aquatic life, suggests contamination.
2. **Air Quality**:
    ◦ Fallout particles may cause hazy or dust-filled air, especially immediately after a nuclear event.

Technical Indicators

1. **Radiation Detectors**:
    ◦ Use Geiger counters or radiation survey meters to measure levels before entering an area.
    ◦ Regularly test personal dosimeters to track cumulative exposure.
2. **Electronic Tools**:
    ◦ Smartphone apps and online databases may provide radiation readings in specific locations.
    ◦ Portable spectrometers identify specific isotopes in the environment.

Strategies for Avoiding Radioactive Zones

1. Route Planning

- Study fallout patterns and map safer routes before traveling.
- Avoid paths through valleys, downwind areas, or regions with known "hot spots."

2. Timing

- Wait for radiation levels to decrease before entering moderately contaminated areas.
- Limit outdoor activities to early morning or late evening to avoid UV and radiation synergy.

3. Protective Measures

- Wear protective clothing and masks when traveling through or near contaminated zones.
- Carry radiation detection tools to monitor exposure levels in real time.

4. Shelter Selection

- Prioritize well-shielded shelters in low-contamination areas.
- Avoid basements or ground-level structures in flood-prone regions, where water may carry fallout particles.

Long-Term Considerations

1. **Resettlement:**
   - Relocate to low-contamination zones as radiation levels decline and resources become available.
   - Test soil, water, and air quality before establishing long-term settlements.
2. **Monitoring:**
   - Regularly check radiation levels in previously contaminated areas to track changes.
   - Use personal dosimeters to ensure cumulative exposure remains within safe limits.
3. **Community Collaboration:**
   - Share maps and data with neighbors to improve collective understanding of radioactive zones.
   - Establish communication networks to report new risks or safe areas.

Psychological Resilience in Navigating Zones

1. **Confidence Through Knowledge:**
   - Understanding radioactive zones and how to navigate them reduces fear and panic.
2. **Teamwork and Planning:**
   - Work with trusted individuals to plan safe routes and share responsibilities.
3. **Adaptability:**
   - Stay flexible and ready to adjust plans based on new information or changing conditions.

Final Thoughts

Radioactive zones are a complex and dynamic challenge in a post-nuclear environment, but with the right tools, knowledge, and preparation, you can navigate them safely. By creating detailed survival maps, recognizing environmental and technical indicators, and adapting to changing conditions, you can minimize exposure and build a sustainable future in even the most challenging circumstances. Knowledge is your greatest ally in a world shaped by radiation—use it wisely to protect yourself and your community.

The New Weather Patterns: Living with Post-War Climate Change

In the aftermath of a nuclear war, weather patterns will shift dramatically, creating new challenges for survival and adaptation. The release of massive amounts of soot, ash, and debris into the atmosphere, combined with widespread environmental damage, will likely lead to a phenomenon known as **nuclear winter** and other long-term climate changes. Understanding these changes and their impact on the environment, agriculture, and daily life is essential for surviving and thriving in a transformed world.

The Causes of Post-War Climate Change

1. **Soot and Smoke in the Atmosphere**:
   - Nuclear explosions and subsequent fires release millions of tons of soot and ash into the upper atmosphere.
   - These particles block sunlight, significantly reducing surface temperatures.
2. **Destruction of the Ozone Layer**:
   - High-altitude explosions release nitrogen oxides that deplete the ozone layer, increasing UV radiation at the surface.
3. **Altered Weather Systems**:
   - The cooling effect of reduced sunlight disrupts global wind patterns and jet streams, leading to erratic and extreme weather.
4. **Radioactive Fallout**:
   - Fallout particles interact with the atmosphere, influencing precipitation patterns and spreading contamination.

Characteristics of Post-War Weather Patterns

1. **Nuclear Winter**:
   - Global temperatures drop significantly due to blocked sunlight.
   - Cold conditions persist for months or years, depending on the scale of the war.
2. **Increased Precipitation Variability**:
   - Some regions may experience prolonged droughts, while others face heavy, radioactive rainfall (known as "black rain").
3. **Higher UV Levels**:
   - Depletion of the ozone layer increases the intensity of UV radiation, posing risks to humans, animals, and crops.
4. **Unpredictable Seasons**:
   - Traditional seasonal patterns may disappear, with extended winters, shortened summers, and unpredictable growing conditions.

Adapting to New Climate Challenges

1. Surviving the Cold

- **Insulate Shelters**:
  - Use layers of blankets, plastic sheeting, and insulation materials to retain heat.

- Seal windows and doors to prevent drafts.
- **Alternative Heating**:
    - Use wood stoves, solar heaters, or improvised thermal mass heaters.
    - Stockpile firewood or other fuels for long-term use.
- **Clothing**:
    - Wear multiple layers, including thermals and windproof outer garments.
    - Focus on covering extremities with gloves, hats, and thick socks.

2. Managing Precipitation

- **Water Collection**:
    - Use covered containers to collect rainwater while avoiding black rain.
    - Purify all collected water to remove radioactive contaminants.
- **Drainage Systems**:
    - Build trenches or barriers to direct water away from living areas and prevent flooding.
- **Protecting Shelter**:
    - Reinforce roofs and walls against heavy snowfall or rain to prevent collapse or leaks.

3. UV Radiation Protection

- **Outdoor Activity**:
    - Minimize time spent outdoors during peak sunlight hours.
    - Wear UV-protective clothing, hats, and sunglasses to shield skin and eyes.
- **Indoor Safety**:
    - Install UV-blocking films on windows to reduce exposure indoors.
- **Sunscreen Use**:
    - Apply sunscreen with high SPF to exposed skin, even during colder months.

Adapting Agriculture to New Conditions

1. **Growing Crops in Cold Climates**:
    - Focus on cold-resistant crops like kale, spinach, and root vegetables (carrots, potatoes).
    - Use greenhouses, cold frames, or indoor grow lights to extend growing seasons.
2. **Managing Drought or Flooding**:
    - Build raised beds or terraces to improve drainage in flood-prone areas.
    - Use drip irrigation or mulching techniques to conserve water in dry conditions.
3. **Protecting Against UV Radiation**:
    - Install shade cloths over outdoor crops to limit UV damage.
    - Prioritize crops with thick skins or leaves that resist radiation.
4. **Soil Remediation**:
    - Test and treat soil for radioactive contamination before planting.
    - Use clean soil in raised beds or containers for safer farming.

Wildlife and Ecosystem Changes

1. **Animal Migration**:
    ◦ Changes in weather may force wildlife to migrate, potentially bringing new pests or predators to your area.
    ◦ Monitor local fauna and adapt strategies for hunting or defense accordingly.
2. **Loss of Pollinators**:
    ◦ Declines in bee and butterfly populations may require manual pollination of crops.
    ◦ Consider attracting or protecting alternative pollinators like flies or moths.
3. **New Species Behavior**:
    ◦ Some species may adapt to harsher conditions, altering the balance of local ecosystems.

Psychological Impacts of Changing Weather

1. **Dealing with Prolonged Cold**:
    ◦ Combat seasonal depression with light therapy using battery-powered lamps.
    ◦ Establish routines and activities that keep morale high during long winters.
2. **Coping with Uncertainty**:
    ◦ Focus on preparedness and flexibility to adapt to sudden weather changes.
    ◦ Share experiences and solutions with your community to foster resilience.
3. **Finding Opportunities**:
    ◦ Use time indoors to develop new skills, maintain social bonds, and build resource networks.

Long-Term Planning for Post-War Climate Change

1. **Rebuilding Infrastructure**:
    ◦ Collaborate with local communities to repair or build climate-resilient shelters and farming systems.
    ◦ Establish storage facilities for food, water, and other essentials to buffer against weather disruptions.
2. **Monitoring Climate Changes**:
    ◦ Keep detailed records of temperature, precipitation, and seasonal shifts to identify patterns.
    ◦ Use this information to refine survival strategies and resource planning.
3. **Diversifying Resources**:
    ◦ Develop backup plans for food and water supplies in case primary sources fail.
    ◦ Experiment with alternative energy sources like wind or solar for heating and electricity.

Final Thoughts

Living with post-war climate change requires adaptability, ingenuity, and a willingness to embrace new survival strategies. While the challenges are immense, understanding the causes and effects of altered weather patterns empowers you to anticipate risks and take proactive measures. By focusing on shelter, agriculture, and psychological resilience, you can navigate the complexities of a transformed climate and lay the foundation for long-term recovery and stability.

Managing Limited Resources: Making Every Drop and Bite Count

In a post-nuclear world, managing limited resources is a fundamental survival skill. With disrupted supply chains, contaminated environments, and uncertain renewal of essential goods, making the most of every drop of water and bite of food becomes critical. This chapter explores practical strategies for rationing, conservation, and sustainable use of resources to ensure survival and resilience over the long term.

Understanding the Resource Challenges

1. **Water Scarcity**:
   - Fallout-contaminated water sources require purification, limiting immediate availability.
   - Rainfall may carry radioactive particles, further reducing safe water options.
2. **Food Insecurity**:
   - Crops, livestock, and stored food may be tainted by fallout.
   - Reduced sunlight and disrupted growing seasons limit agricultural productivity.
3. **Energy and Supplies**:
   - Power outages and lack of fuel complicate cooking, heating, and preservation.
   - Limited access to essential tools and materials requires careful maintenance and reuse.

Strategies for Managing Water

1. Collecting and Storing Water

- **Rainwater Harvesting**:
  - Use tarps, gutters, or other clean surfaces to collect rainwater.
  - Avoid collecting during initial fallout periods and test for contamination before use.
- **Storage**:
  - Store water in sealed, durable containers to prevent contamination and evaporation.
  - Rotate stored water periodically to maintain freshness.

2. Purification Techniques

- **Boiling**:
  - Boil water for at least 1-3 minutes to kill pathogens, but note that boiling does not remove radioactive particles.
- **Filtration**:
  - Use portable water filters with activated carbon to remove impurities and reduce some radioactive isotopes.
- **Chemical Treatment**:
  - Treat water with iodine tablets or bleach (sodium hypochlorite) for biological safety.
- **Distillation**:
  - Create a solar still or use heat distillation to separate clean water from contaminants.

3. Conservation Methods

- Reuse greywater from washing for non-potable needs, like cleaning or irrigation.
- Minimize waste by collecting water from cooking or condensation for reuse.

Strategies for Managing Food

1. Rationing and Meal Planning

- **Portion Control**:
    - Distribute food evenly among family members, prioritizing nutritional needs.
    - Divide meals into small, frequent portions to sustain energy throughout the day.
- **Prioritize Perishables**:
    - Consume fresh or perishable foods first, reserving preserved items for later use.
- **Nutritional Balance**:
    - Focus on high-calorie, nutrient-dense foods such as grains, beans, and nuts to maximize energy and health.

2. Preservation Techniques

- **Drying**:
    - Air-dry or use low heat to preserve fruits, vegetables, and meats.
- **Canning**:
    - Pressure-can or water-bath can foods to extend their shelf life.
- **Salting and Smoking**:
    - Use salt or smoke to preserve meats and fish in the absence of refrigeration.
- **Fermentation**:
    - Ferment vegetables like cabbage (sauerkraut) or cucumbers (pickles) to create long-lasting, probiotic-rich foods.

3. Growing and Foraging

- **Indoor Gardening**:
    - Use hydroponic or container systems to grow vegetables, herbs, and microgreens indoors with controlled conditions.
- **Foraging**:
    - Learn to identify edible wild plants and fungi in your area.
    - Avoid foraging in heavily contaminated zones or near fallout hotspots.

Maximizing Energy Efficiency

1. Cooking and Heating

- **Efficient Stoves**:
    - Use rocket stoves or solar cookers that require minimal fuel.

- **Low-Energy Cooking:**
  - Prepare one-pot meals or slow-cook foods to reduce fuel consumption.
- **Heat Conservation:**
  - Insulate cooking pots with towels or improvised thermal boxes to retain heat.

2. Preservation without Refrigeration

- **Root Cellars:**
  - Store root vegetables and hardy produce in cool, dark, and ventilated spaces.
- **Evaporative Cooling:**
  - Use clay pots or damp cloths around containers to create a cooling effect.

Maintaining Tools and Supplies

1. **Reusing and Repurposing:**
   - Convert old clothing into rags, bandages, or patchwork materials.
   - Reuse containers for storage or water collection.
2. **Repairing:**
   - Keep tools sharp and functional with regular maintenance.
   - Learn basic sewing, carpentry, and metalwork for DIY repairs.
3. **Bartering and Sharing:**
   - Trade excess resources or skills with neighbors to acquire needed items.
   - Establish community agreements to pool resources and avoid duplication.

Waste Management for Sustainability

1. **Reducing Waste:**
   - Minimize scraps by using all parts of food (e.g., bones for broth, vegetable peels for compost).
   - Plan meals to reduce leftovers and spoilage.
2. **Composting:**
   - Create a compost system for organic waste, enriching soil for future gardening.
   - Ensure compost is free of radioactive contaminants by testing inputs.
3. **Sanitary Disposal:**
   - Dispose of waste in sealed bags or pits to prevent pest attraction and contamination.
   - Use lime or ash to neutralize waste odors and pathogens.

Psychological and Social Aspects of Resource Management

1. **Psychological Resilience:**
   - Focus on small victories, like successfully stretching food supplies or purifying water, to boost morale.
   - Involve all family members in resource management tasks to share responsibility and foster teamwork.
2. **Community Cooperation:**
   - Share knowledge and resources with trusted neighbors to enhance collective survival.

    ° Develop community gardens or shared resource centers to maximize efficiency.

Planning for Long-Term Sustainability

1. **Stockpiling Essentials**:
    - Build reserves of long-lasting foods (rice, beans, canned goods) and essential tools.
    - Include water purification supplies, seeds, and spare parts for critical equipment.
2. **Rotating Supplies**:
    - Regularly use and replace stored items to maintain freshness and usability.
    - Track inventory to avoid shortages and waste.
3. **Adapting Practices**:
    - Continuously refine techniques for water collection, food preservation, and energy use based on changing conditions.

Final Thoughts

Managing limited resources is not just about survival—it's about thriving in the face of adversity. By prioritizing conservation, embracing sustainability, and fostering resilience, you can make every drop of water and bite of food count. These strategies ensure not only survival but also hope and stability in a challenging world. With careful planning and resourcefulness, you can navigate scarcity and build a foundation for a better future.

Renewable Energy for Survival: Harnessing Post-War Resources

In a post-nuclear world, traditional energy sources like electricity, gas, and fuel may be unavailable for months or even years. Renewable energy becomes a lifeline, enabling survivors to power essential tools, purify water, cook food, and maintain communication. Harnessing post-war resources for energy is not only practical but critical for long-term survival and rebuilding. This chapter explores the potential of renewable energy sources and provides strategies for setting up and utilizing these systems in a resource-scarce environment.

Why Renewable Energy is Essential

1. **Independence from Infrastructure**:
   - With power grids destroyed or unreliable, renewable energy provides self-sufficiency.
   - Solar, wind, and other sources are abundant and not reliant on supply chains.
2. **Sustainability**:
   - Unlike finite fossil fuels, renewable resources regenerate, ensuring a steady energy supply.
3. **Adaptability**:
   - Renewable systems can be scaled to meet individual or community needs.

Renewable Energy Options for Survival

1. Solar Power

- **Advantages**:
  - Solar panels are portable, durable, and effective even in partial sunlight.
  - Easy to set up with minimal maintenance.
- **Setup**:
  - Use photovoltaic (PV) panels to capture sunlight and convert it into electricity.
  - Pair panels with batteries to store energy for nighttime use.
- **Applications**:
  - Power lights, radios, water pumps, and small appliances.
  - Charge essential devices like communication equipment and Geiger counters.

2. Wind Energy

- **Advantages**:
  - Effective in areas with consistent wind patterns, including coastal or open plains.
  - Can operate day and night, unlike solar panels.
- **Setup**:
  - Construct small wind turbines using salvaged materials like PVC pipes, bike parts, and car alternators.
  - Install turbines in open, elevated locations to maximize wind capture.
- **Applications**:
  - Generate electricity for larger loads, such as heating or water filtration systems.

3. Hydropower

- **Advantages**:
    - Provides continuous power in areas with flowing rivers or streams.
    - Simple to maintain once installed.
- **Setup**:
    - Build small water wheels or turbines to harness energy from water flow.
    - Channel water through pipes to create controlled flow for optimal power generation.
- **Applications**:
    - Ideal for long-term settlements near water sources.

4. Biomass Energy

- **Advantages**:
    - Uses readily available organic materials like wood, crop waste, or animal dung.
    - Produces heat for cooking and heating.
- **Setup**:
    - Build a biomass stove or digester to convert organic material into usable energy.
    - Use methane from anaerobic digestion to fuel stoves or small generators.
- **Applications**:
    - Heat shelters, cook food, and generate biofuel.

5. Hand-Generated Power

- **Advantages**:
    - Requires no external resources, making it highly reliable in emergencies.
- **Setup**:
    - Use hand-crank generators or pedal-powered systems to produce electricity manually.
- **Applications**:
    - Charge small devices or power LED lights in low-energy scenarios.

Building and Utilizing Renewable Systems

1. Scavenging and Salvaging

- Collect solar panels, batteries, inverters, and wiring from abandoned homes, vehicles, or facilities.
- Repurpose parts like alternators, motors, and blades for DIY wind or water turbines.

2. Energy Storage

- Use deep-cycle batteries to store energy from solar, wind, or hydro systems.
- Maintain batteries by keeping them charged and stored in cool, dry places.

3. DIY Renewable Systems

- **Solar Cookers**:
    - Create reflective solar ovens using aluminum foil and cardboard to focus sunlight for cooking.
- **Wind Turbines**:
    - Build small windmills with salvaged materials to generate power for lights or small devices.
- **Biogas Digesters**:
    - Construct systems to produce methane gas from organic waste for cooking and heating.

4. Maintenance and Repair

- Regularly clean solar panels and turbine blades to ensure efficiency.
- Inspect wiring and connections for wear, replacing damaged components promptly.

Prioritizing Energy Needs

1. **Essential Uses**:
    - Focus on powering critical devices like water purifiers, medical equipment, and communication tools.
    - Allocate energy for lighting and heating to maintain safety and comfort.
2. **Conservation**:
    - Use energy-efficient devices such as LED lights and low-power appliances.
    - Limit usage to essential times, storing surplus energy in batteries.

Challenges and Solutions

1. **Limited Resources**:
    - Use DIY solutions to build energy systems from salvaged materials.
    - Collaborate with neighbors to share energy resources and knowledge.
2. **Unpredictable Weather**:
    - Combine energy sources (solar, wind, and biomass) to mitigate reliance on one system.
    - Store energy during favorable conditions to use during periods of low output.
3. **Skill Gaps**:
    - Learn basic electrical and mechanical skills to install and maintain renewable systems.
    - Share skills within a community to build collective expertise.

Scaling Renewable Energy for Communities

1. **Shared Systems**:
    - Build larger solar arrays, wind turbines, or hydro systems to power multiple shelters or community centers.
    - Distribute energy equitably among members based on needs.
2. **Community Workshops**:
    - Organize training sessions to teach residents how to construct and maintain renewable systems.

- ◦ Pool resources for collective projects, reducing individual costs and efforts.
3. **Resource Management**:
    - ◦ Develop energy-sharing schedules or rationing plans to avoid overuse or conflicts.

Psychological and Practical Benefits

1. **Empowerment**:
    - ◦ Renewable energy systems provide a sense of control and independence.
    - ◦ Creating and maintaining these systems fosters confidence and skill development.
2. **Stability**:
    - ◦ Reliable energy sources reduce stress and improve quality of life in uncertain times.
    - ◦ Access to light, heat, and power supports mental and physical health.
3. **Hope for Recovery**:
    - ◦ Renewable energy lays the groundwork for rebuilding and future development.

Final Thoughts

Harnessing renewable energy in a post-war world is not just a matter of survival but a step toward resilience and recovery. By combining resourcefulness, creativity, and collaboration, you can create sustainable energy solutions that power your needs and sustain your community. In the face of adversity, renewable energy is a beacon of hope and a foundation for rebuilding a better future.

Adapting to a Hostile Environment: Living with Radiation

Living in a post-nuclear world requires adapting to an environment where radiation is a persistent threat. While radioactive fallout diminishes over time, residual contamination in air, water, soil, and food demands ongoing vigilance. Adapting to this hostile environment involves understanding radiation, minimizing exposure, and implementing protective measures to ensure long-term survival. This chapter explores strategies for living with radiation and creating a sustainable, safer existence.

Understanding Radiation

1. **Types of Radiation**:
   - **Alpha Radiation**: Low penetration, blocked by skin or clothing, but harmful if inhaled or ingested.
   - **Beta Radiation**: Can penetrate skin and cause burns but is stopped by dense clothing or barriers.
   - **Gamma Radiation**: Highly penetrating, requiring dense materials like lead, concrete, or water for shielding.
2. **Sources in a Post-Nuclear World**:
   - Fallout particles settling on surfaces, plants, and animals.
   - Contaminated water and food.
   - Persistent radioactive isotopes like cesium-137 and strontium-90.
3. **Radiation Measurement**:
   - Use Geiger counters or dosimeters to measure radiation levels in your environment.
   - Track cumulative exposure to stay within safe limits.

Minimizing Radiation Exposure

1. **Sheltering**:
   - **Shielding**: Use dense materials (earth, sandbags, concrete) to create barriers against gamma radiation.
   - **Location**: Stay indoors, especially during initial fallout periods, and choose basements or central rooms for maximum shielding.
   - **Ventilation**: Use HEPA filters or improvised air filtration systems to remove radioactive particles from indoor air.
2. **Protective Clothing**:
   - Wear long-sleeve shirts, pants, gloves, and masks when venturing outdoors.
   - Use waterproof or plastic-coated outer layers to prevent fallout particles from clinging to fabric.
   - Wash clothing separately and frequently to remove contamination.
3. **Time and Distance**:
   - Limit time spent in high-radiation areas to reduce exposure.
   - Increase distance from radiation sources, as intensity decreases significantly with distance.

Decontamination Practices

1. **Personal Hygiene**:
   - Wash exposed skin with soap and clean water immediately after outdoor activities.
   - Avoid scrubbing too hard to prevent particles from entering abrasions or wounds.
   - Rinse hair thoroughly without using conditioner, as it can bind fallout particles.
2. **Clothing and Equipment**:
   - Remove and seal contaminated clothing in plastic bags before entering clean areas.
   - Decontaminate tools and equipment by rinsing with clean water or wiping with damp cloths.
3. **Living Spaces**:
   - Clean surfaces regularly with damp cloths to trap and remove fallout particles.
   - Avoid shaking out rugs or fabrics, which can resuspend particles into the air.

Managing Contaminated Resources

1. **Water**:
   - Purify all water with distillation, filtration, or chemical treatment before use.
   - Test water sources regularly for radioactive contamination.
   - Use covered containers to collect and store clean rainwater, avoiding collection during fallout periods.
2. **Food**:
   - Grow crops in uncontaminated soil using raised beds or indoor systems.
   - Wash or peel all fruits and vegetables before consumption.
   - Avoid consuming wild animals or livestock exposed to fallout unless tested for contamination.
3. **Soil and Agriculture**:
   - Test soil for radiation levels before planting.
   - Remediate contaminated soil using clean topsoil, barriers, or phytoremediation techniques.
   - Rotate crops to reduce the accumulation of radioactive isotopes in edible plants.

Monitoring Radiation Levels

1. **Tools and Devices**:
   - Use Geiger counters to measure ambient radiation in your area.
   - Employ dosimeters to track personal exposure over time.
2. **Community Networks**:
   - Share radiation readings with neighbors or local groups to create comprehensive maps of contaminated areas.
   - Establish safe zones for communal activities.
3. **Regular Testing**:
   - Test air, water, and soil frequently, especially after rain, which can concentrate fallout particles.

Long-Term Adaptation

1. **Developing Resilient Habits**:
    ◦ Build routines around decontamination, protective measures, and regular monitoring.
    ◦ Educate all family members on radiation safety protocols.
2. **Sustainable Living**:
    ◦ Invest in renewable energy sources like solar or wind to reduce dependency on contaminated fuel sources.
    ◦ Create indoor gardening systems for food production in controlled environments.
3. **Psychological Resilience**:
    ◦ Maintain mental health through structured routines, community interaction, and stress-reducing activities.
    ◦ Focus on small victories, such as successfully reducing exposure or growing clean food.

Psychological Challenges and Coping Strategies

1. **Fear and Uncertainty**:
    ◦ Counteract fear with knowledge about radiation and clear action plans for safety.
    ◦ Limit exposure to misinformation or panic-inducing rumors.
2. **Isolation**:
    ◦ Foster connections with neighbors or trusted groups to create a sense of community.
    ◦ Engage in shared projects like building shelters or planting community gardens.
3. **Morale Boosters**:
    ◦ Celebrate milestones, such as successfully harvesting clean crops or improving shelter conditions.
    ◦ Allow time for recreation and relaxation to maintain emotional balance.

Community Collaboration for Adaptation

1. **Shared Resources**:
    ◦ Pool clean water, uncontaminated food, and protective gear with trusted neighbors.
    ◦ Establish communal shelters or safe zones for larger groups.
2. **Knowledge Sharing**:
    ◦ Teach others how to use radiation detection tools, build protective structures, and decontaminate resources.
    ◦ Share maps of safe and contaminated areas to improve collective survival efforts.
3. **Collective Projects**:
    ◦ Work together to construct radiation shields, water purification systems, and renewable energy setups.

Preparing for the Future

1. **Education**:
    ◦ Learn and teach basic survival skills, including radiation safety, first aid, and sustainable farming.
    ◦ Keep a library of resources on radiation science and survival techniques.
2. **Innovation**:
    ◦ Experiment with new methods for decontamination, resource conservation, and energy production.
    ◦ Encourage creativity in problem-solving to adapt to changing conditions.
3. **Monitoring Progress**:
    ◦ Track improvements in radiation levels and adapt strategies as areas become safer.
    ◦ Establish long-term goals for rebuilding and expanding safe zones.

Final Thoughts

Living with radiation is challenging, but it is possible to adapt and thrive through careful planning, vigilance, and community collaboration. By minimizing exposure, decontaminating effectively, and managing resources wisely, you can build a sustainable way of life in a hostile environment. With resilience, ingenuity, and determination, you can not only survive but lay the groundwork for recovery and renewal.

The Role of Technology in Survival: Tools You Can Use

Technology plays a crucial role in survival after a nuclear war, providing tools to monitor, protect, and sustain life in a hostile environment. From simple gadgets to advanced devices, the right technology can help you adapt, manage resources, and minimize risks from radiation and other dangers. This chapter explores essential tools, their applications, and how to integrate technology into your survival strategy.

Why Technology Matters

1. **Enhanced Safety**:
    - Radiation detection tools alert you to hazardous areas and materials.
    - Protective equipment and filtration systems reduce exposure to harmful elements.
2. **Resource Management**:
    - Devices help purify water, store energy, and monitor food safety.
3. **Communication and Navigation**:
    - Technology ensures you stay connected, informed, and oriented in a disrupted world.
4. **Sustainability**:
    - Renewable energy systems and indoor farming technologies provide long-term solutions for survival.

Essential Tools for Survival

1. Radiation Detection

- **Geiger Counters**:
    - Measure radiation levels in the air, water, and soil.
    - Essential for identifying "hot spots" and assessing safety.
- **Dosimeters**:
    - Track cumulative radiation exposure over time to ensure you stay within safe limits.
- **Radiosensitive Film Badges**:
    - Wearable devices for monitoring personal exposure to radiation.

2. Water Purification

- **Portable Water Filters**:
    - Use activated carbon and ceramic filters to remove contaminants.
    - Some models can reduce certain radioactive isotopes.
- **UV Purifiers**:
    - Use ultraviolet light to kill bacteria and viruses in water.
- **Distillation Systems**:
    - Separate clean water from impurities and radioactive particles through heat.

3. Energy Solutions

- **Solar Panels**:
  - Provide renewable power for lighting, cooking, and small devices.
- **Portable Power Banks**:
  - Store electricity for essential gadgets like radios and phones.
- **Hand-Crank Generators**:
  - Generate electricity manually for charging small devices.
- **Wind Turbines**:
  - Capture wind energy to power shelters or larger systems.

4. Protective Equipment

- **Respirators and Masks**:
  - Filter out fallout particles and other airborne contaminants.
  - Ensure a supply of replaceable filters.
- **Radiation Shields**:
  - Portable lead or dense material shields for temporary shelter or working in high-radiation areas.
- **Protective Clothing**:
  - Waterproof outer layers to prevent fallout from adhering to skin or clothing.

5. Food Safety and Production

- **Soil Testers**:
  - Detect radiation and chemical contamination in soil before planting.
- **Hydroponic Systems**:
  - Grow food indoors using nutrient-rich water instead of soil.
- **Dehydrators**:
  - Preserve fruits, vegetables, and meats for long-term storage.

6. Communication

- **Two-Way Radios**:
  - Maintain contact with family or community members in areas without cellular service.
- **Shortwave Radios**:
  - Receive news and emergency broadcasts from distant locations.
- **Signal Beacons**:
  - Attract rescuers or signal your location in emergencies.

7. Navigation

- **GPS Devices**:
  - Provide accurate location data and route planning.
- **Compass and Maps**:

- **Altimeters**:
  - Measure elevation changes, useful for avoiding fallout-accumulating valleys.

8. Medical Technology

- **First-Aid Kits with Digital Monitors**:
  - Include tools like pulse oximeters and electronic thermometers.
- **Portable Diagnostic Devices**:
  - Test for radiation poisoning symptoms or monitor chronic health conditions.
- **Sterilizers**:
  - UV or steam-based devices to clean medical tools and supplies.

Building a Survival Tech Kit

1. **Prioritize Versatility**:
   - Choose multi-functional devices that serve multiple purposes, like solar chargers with built-in lights.
2. **Durability Matters**:
   - Opt for rugged, waterproof, and shock-resistant tools built for harsh conditions.
3. **Power Efficiency**:
   - Focus on energy-efficient tools to maximize the use of limited power resources.
4. **Maintain and Repair**:
   - Include repair kits for critical devices and learn basic maintenance skills.

DIY and Improvised Technology

1. **Homemade Filters**:
   - Build water filters using sand, charcoal, and gravel in a layered system.
2. **Solar Cookers**:
   - Construct reflectors using aluminum foil and cardboard to cook food or boil water.
3. **Improvised Radios**:
   - Assemble basic AM/FM receivers with salvaged components.
4. **Makeshift Generators**:
   - Repurpose car alternators or bike parts to create wind or pedal-powered generators.

Integrating Technology into Daily Survival

1. **Monitoring and Testing**:
   - Regularly test radiation levels and resource safety to guide decision-making.
   - Rotate devices like dosimeters among family members for comprehensive exposure tracking.
2. **Energy Planning**:
   - Schedule energy-intensive tasks during peak solar or wind periods.
   - Use power banks to store excess energy for night-time or emergencies.

1. **Community Sharing**:
   - Share advanced tools like radiation detectors or water purifiers with neighbors to maximize their utility.
   - Collaborate on renewable energy projects, such as shared solar arrays or wind turbines.

Challenges and Solutions

1. **Limited Access**:
   - Salvage abandoned buildings, vehicles, or equipment for tools and parts.
   - Barter with others to acquire essential devices.
2. **Device Maintenance**:
   - Learn basic electronics repair and keep spare parts for high-use devices.
   - Protect devices from moisture, dust, and physical damage.
3. **Skill Gaps**:
   - Train yourself and others in operating and maintaining survival technologies.
   - Use online resources or community knowledge to learn critical skills before they're needed.

Psychological and Practical Benefits

1. **Peace of Mind**:
   - Access to technology reduces uncertainty and fear, allowing you to focus on problem-solving.
2. **Efficiency**:
   - Tools simplify tasks like water purification, farming, and energy production, conserving your time and effort.
3. **Community Resilience**:
   - Sharing tools and skills fosters collaboration and strengthens social bonds.

Final Thoughts

Technology is an invaluable ally in surviving a post-nuclear world, offering solutions for safety, resource management, and communication. By choosing the right tools, learning to use them effectively, and integrating them into daily life, you can enhance your chances of survival and adapt to the challenges of a hostile environment. With ingenuity and determination, even limited technology can make a significant difference in your journey toward resilience and recovery.

Making Do with Less: Survival Skills for Limited Resources

Surviving with limited resources requires adaptability, creativity, and a deep understanding of how to maximize what you have. When access to essentials like food, water, and shelter is constrained, survival hinges on using skills to stretch resources, repurpose materials, and find sustainable solutions. This chapter explores practical strategies and techniques to help you thrive in scarcity.

Mindset for Scarcity Survival

1. **Adaptability**:
    - Embrace flexibility in how you approach daily needs and challenges.
    - Be open to alternative solutions for common problems.
2. **Resourcefulness**:
    - View all items as potentially useful. Repurpose and salvage materials whenever possible.
    - Focus on turning perceived waste into assets.
3. **Prioritization**:
    - Allocate resources to the most critical survival needs: water, food, shelter, and safety.

Conserving and Managing Resources

1. Water

- **Collection**:
    - Use tarps, gutters, or plastic sheeting to collect rainwater.
    - Condense and collect water vapor from plants using plastic bags or solar stills.
- **Conservation**:
    - Reuse greywater for tasks like cleaning tools or flushing waste.
    - Limit water usage to drinking and essential hygiene.
- **Purification**:
    - Use boiling, filtration, or distillation to ensure water is safe.

2. Food

- **Rationing**:
    - Divide food into small portions to ensure it lasts as long as possible.
    - Prioritize high-calorie, nutrient-dense foods for energy.
- **Preservation**:
    - Dehydrate fruits and vegetables to extend shelf life.
    - Salt or smoke meats to prevent spoilage without refrigeration.
- **Foraging**:
    - Learn to identify edible wild plants, berries, and fungi in your area.
    - Avoid areas with potential radiation contamination.

3. Energy

- **Efficient Cooking**:
    - Use rocket stoves or solar cookers to minimize fuel consumption.
    - Prepare one-pot meals to reduce cooking time and energy use.
- **Heating**:
    - Insulate shelters with layered materials like blankets, newspaper, or leaves.
    - Use body heat or group sleeping arrangements to stay warm.

Repurposing and Improvising

1. **Tools**:
    - Convert scrap metal into knives, hooks, or digging implements.
    - Fashion basic tools from wood, stone, or other natural materials.
2. **Clothing**:
    - Patch worn clothing with salvaged fabric or other materials.
    - Use plastic sheeting or trash bags as makeshift rain gear.
3. **Shelter**:
    - Construct shelters with available materials like wood, tarps, or debris.
    - Reinforce existing structures with sandbags or packed earth for insulation and protection.
4. **Containers**:
    - Repurpose cans, jars, or bottles for storage, cooking, or water collection.
    - Use hollowed-out logs or shells as improvised containers.

Sustainable Practices for Limited Resources

1. **Growing Food**:
    - Establish a small garden using salvaged seeds and nutrient-rich soil.
    - Grow fast-maturing crops like radishes, spinach, or beans to ensure a steady food supply.
2. **Livestock**:
    - Raise low-maintenance animals like chickens, rabbits, or ducks for meat, eggs, and fertilizer.
    - Use food scraps to feed animals and reduce waste.
3. **Waste Reduction**:
    - Compost organic waste to create fertilizer for gardening.
    - Find creative ways to reuse or repurpose non-organic waste.

Essential Survival Skills

1. **Fire Making**:
    - Use flint and steel, a magnifying glass, or improvised tools like a bow drill to start fires.
    - Collect and dry tinder like bark, grass, or cloth to ensure you're always prepared.
2. **Knot Tying**:
    - Learn basic knots like the square knot, bowline, and clove hitch for securing shelters, traps, or tools.

1. **First Aid:**
    ◦ Use natural remedies like plantain for cuts or burns and willow bark for pain relief.
    ◦ Create improvised splints or slings from sticks and cloth.

1. **Navigation:**
    ◦ Use the sun, stars, or natural landmarks to find your way without a compass.
    ◦ Learn to read animal trails or water flows to locate resources.

Psychological Resilience

1. **Stay Calm:**
    ◦ In moments of scarcity, panic wastes energy and resources. Focus on immediate priorities.
2. **Set Goals:**
    ◦ Break tasks into achievable steps, like collecting a set amount of water or securing shelter for the night.
3. **Build Community:**
    ◦ Share resources and skills with others to increase collective survival chances.
4. **Celebrate Success:**
    ◦ Acknowledge small victories, such as finding food or improving your shelter, to boost morale.

Collaboration and Bartering

1. **Share Resources:**
    ◦ Pool items like tools, seeds, or knowledge with neighbors or fellow survivors.
    ◦ Build trust by offering assistance or sharing surplus resources.
2. **Trade Skills:**
    ◦ Offer skills like repair work, medical aid, or hunting in exchange for needed supplies.
    ◦ Form small groups to divide labor and specialize in specific tasks.

Preparing for the Future

1. **Stockpiling:**
    ◦ Create a reserve of long-lasting supplies like dried foods, batteries, and first-aid materials.
2. **Skill Building:**
    ◦ Practice essential survival skills regularly to ensure confidence and efficiency.
3. **Continuous Learning:**
    ◦ Learn from successes and failures to refine your strategies for managing limited resources.

Final Thoughts

Making do with less is a test of ingenuity and resilience. By developing essential survival skills, repurposing materials, and adopting sustainable practices, you can stretch scarce resources and thrive despite challenges. In a world where every drop of water and bite of food counts, resourcefulness and creativity become the ultimate tools for survival. With determination and adaptability, you can navigate scarcity and build a foundation for stability and recovery.

Emergency Communication: Staying Connected When It Matters Most

In a post-nuclear world, staying connected is crucial for survival, safety, and rebuilding. With traditional communication infrastructure likely destroyed or unreliable, emergency communication systems become the lifeline for sharing information, coordinating efforts, and seeking help. This chapter explores tools, strategies, and techniques to maintain communication when it matters most.

Why Communication is Essential

1. **Safety and Security**:
     - Alert others to dangers like radiation hotspots, hostile individuals, or environmental hazards.
     - Coordinate rescue or evacuation efforts.
2. **Resource Sharing**:
     - Exchange critical information about water, food, and safe zones.
     - Organize community efforts for mutual support.
3. **Psychological Support**:
     - Maintain connections with loved ones to combat isolation and fear.
     - Foster a sense of normalcy and hope in a challenging environment.

Communication Tools and Their Uses

1. Two-Way Radios

- **Advantages**:
     - Operate without cellular networks or internet.
     - Compact, durable, and easy to use.
- **Best Uses**:
     - Short-range communication within a community or group.
     - Coordinating efforts during travel or emergencies.

2. HAM Radios

- **Advantages**:
     - Long-range communication; can reach across continents in some cases.
     - Access to emergency frequencies and global networks.
- **Best Uses**:
     - Receiving critical updates from other survivors or emergency services.
     - Broadcasting distress signals or coordinating with distant groups.

3. Shortwave Radios

- **Advantages:**
  - Receive international broadcasts, including news and emergency updates.
  - Do not require internet or cell towers.
- **Best Uses:**
  - Staying informed about broader conditions and developments.
  - Monitoring emergency frequencies.

4. Emergency Beacons

- **Advantages:**
  - Send location-based distress signals to rescuers.
  - Require minimal user interaction.
- **Best Uses:**
  - Marking your location for search and rescue teams.
  - Signaling nearby allies in critical situations.

5. Signal Mirrors and Whistles

- **Advantages:**
  - Simple, reliable, and require no power.
- **Best Uses:**
  - Sending visual or auditory signals over short distances.
  - Attracting attention in open areas or to aircraft.

6. Smartphones (Limited Use)

- **Advantages:**
  - Useful when cellular networks or internet connections are partially functional.
  - Can store maps, emergency plans, and survival guides.
- **Best Uses:**
  - Short-term communication during partial infrastructure recovery.
  - Offline use of stored resources like documents and apps.

Building a Communication Plan

1. **Establish Primary and Backup Methods:**
   - Use two-way radios or HAM radios as your primary tools.
   - Have signal mirrors, whistles, or prearranged visual signals as backups.
2. **Predefine Communication Protocols:**
   - Set specific times for check-ins to conserve battery power.
   - Establish emergency codes or phrases for quick identification of issues.

1. **Map Communication Zones**:
   - Identify areas with strong radio signal reception or less interference.
   - Mark safe zones where communication is easier to maintain.

Enhancing Signal Reliability

1. **Improve Antennas**:
   - Extend radio range by using longer or directional antennas.
   - Salvage materials like copper wire to build makeshift antennas.
2. **Avoid Interference**:
   - Use radios in open spaces away from metal structures or dense forests.
   - Switch frequencies if experiencing interference or jamming.
3. **Optimize Battery Use**:
   - Conserve power by turning off devices when not in use.
   - Use rechargeable batteries and pair with solar chargers for long-term sustainability.

Maintaining Communication Devices

1. **Protect from Elements**:
   - Store radios and other devices in waterproof, shockproof containers.
   - Use silica gel or other desiccants to prevent moisture damage.
2. **Regular Testing**:
   - Test all communication devices weekly to ensure functionality.
   - Replace damaged components, such as antennas or batteries, as needed.
3. **DIY Repairs**:
   - Learn basic electronics repair to fix common issues like broken connections or battery terminals.
   - Keep a toolkit with spare parts, wire, and soldering equipment.

Emergency Communication Techniques

1. **Prearranged Signals**:
   - Use pre-determined patterns (e.g., three whistle blasts for emergency) to signal distress or identify allies.
   - Mark safe routes or meeting points with universal symbols like arrows or circles.
2. **Visual Signals**:
   - Use signal mirrors to reflect sunlight toward rescuers or aircraft.
   - Place large, contrasting objects (e.g., tarps, stones) on open ground for aerial visibility.
3. **Auditory Signals**:
   - Blow whistles in specific patterns to convey messages or attract attention.
   - Bang on metal objects or clap in rhythmic sequences for search teams in confined areas.

Staying Informed

1. **Monitor Emergency Channels**:
    - Tune into government or emergency broadcasts for updates on weather, radiation, or safe zones.
    - Use HAM or shortwave radios to connect with regional or global networks.
2. **Establish Community Networks**:
    - Share information within your group or nearby communities to improve collective awareness.
    - Rotate responsibility for monitoring broadcasts to ensure continuous updates.
3. **Create a Communication Log**:
    - Record messages sent and received, including time, frequency, and content.
    - Use the log to track patterns or follow up on critical information.

Psychological Benefits of Communication

1. **Reduced Isolation**:
    - Staying connected combats feelings of loneliness and fear.
    - Regular check-ins with family or community members foster a sense of belonging.
2. **Increased Confidence**:
    - Access to reliable information helps you make informed decisions.
    - Knowing you can call for help reduces anxiety during emergencies.
3. **Shared Problem-Solving**:
    - Collaboration through communication allows for pooling of resources and expertise.

Long-Term Communication Planning

1. **Stockpile Essential Supplies**:
    - Include spare batteries, cables, and replacement parts in your emergency kit.
    - Keep a backup supply of radios or other devices.
2. **Skill Building**:
    - Learn how to operate HAM radios and obtain a license if possible.
    - Teach others in your group to use communication tools effectively.
3. **Redundancy**:
    - Have multiple communication systems to reduce reliance on a single method.
    - Regularly test and rotate devices to ensure all options remain functional.

Final Thoughts

Emergency communication is more than just a way to stay in touch—it's a lifeline that can mean the difference between safety and danger. By understanding the tools available, maintaining your equipment, and establishing reliable communication plans, you ensure a vital connection to others in a disconnected world. Whether coordinating survival efforts or sharing hope, staying connected truly matters most.

Bartering and Trade: The New Economy in a Broken World

In a post-nuclear world, traditional economic systems will likely collapse, leaving barter and trade as the foundation of a new survival-driven economy. Goods, skills, and knowledge become the new currency, fostering cooperation and resource sharing. Understanding how to navigate this informal economy is critical to securing essentials, building community ties, and thriving in a broken world. This chapter explores the principles of bartering, what to trade, and how to do so safely and effectively.

Why Bartering Matters

1. **Resource Accessibility**:
    - No single person can have everything they need; bartering allows access to scarce resources.
    - Exchanging surplus items for necessities reduces waste and ensures efficient resource use.
2. **Skill Exchange**:
    - Those with specialized skills, such as medical knowledge, mechanics, or farming, can trade their expertise for goods.
3. **Community Building**:
    - Bartering fosters relationships and mutual support, creating networks that enhance collective survival.

What to Barter: High-Value Items and Skills

1. Essential Goods

- **Food**:
    - Long-lasting items like rice, beans, canned goods, and dehydrated food.
    - Seeds for planting, especially non-GMO heirloom varieties.
- **Water**:
    - Purified water in sealed containers or water purification tools like filters and tablets.
- **Medical Supplies**:
    - Bandages, antibiotics, pain relievers, and basic first-aid kits.
- **Fuel and Energy**:
    - Batteries, solar chargers, firewood, and fuel canisters.
- **Clothing and Blankets**:
    - Warm, durable items for protection against the elements.

2. Tools and Equipment

- Hand tools for farming, repair, and construction.
- Multi-tools or knives for everyday use.
- Cooking utensils and portable stoves.

3. Hygiene and Personal Care

- Soap, toothpaste, toothbrushes, and menstrual products.
- Disinfectants like bleach or alcohol for cleaning and medical use.

4. Luxury Items

- Coffee, tea, chocolate, and alcohol, which hold emotional and social value.
- Tobacco or cigarettes for those who use them.

5. Knowledge and Skills

- Medical care: First aid, wound treatment, and basic surgery.
- Mechanical repair: Fixing vehicles, tools, or generators.
- Farming and food preservation: Teaching or assisting with gardening, canning, or dehydrating.
- Security and protection: Offering guidance or assistance with personal safety and shelter fortification.

How to Barter Effectively

1. **Assess Needs and Surplus**:
   - Identify what you need most and what you have to offer.
   - Prioritize items or skills in short supply for trade.
2. **Understand Value**:
   - The value of goods varies by context. For example, water is more valuable in a drought, while tools might hold more importance during planting seasons.
   - Rare or irreplaceable items like medical supplies and seeds often have high trade value.
3. **Negotiate Fairly**:
   - Approach negotiations with honesty and mutual respect.
   - Offer trades that benefit both parties to build trust and encourage future exchanges.
4. **Be Flexible**:
   - Accept alternative goods or services if your preferred item isn't available.
   - Offer bundles (e.g., a tool with instructions for use) to make trades more appealing.

Creating Safe and Reliable Trade Networks

1. **Start Locally**:
   - Trade with neighbors or known individuals to establish trust.
   - Build small trade networks within your immediate community.
2. **Organize Markets**:
   - Create regular trading events where people can exchange goods and services.
   - Set up safe zones for trading with clear rules and security measures.
3. **Develop Communication Channels**:
   - Use radios, word of mouth, or community boards to announce available goods and upcoming trade events.

Bartering Safely

1. **Vet Trading Partners**:
    - Trade first with people you know or those vouched for by trusted individuals.
    - Be cautious of strangers or overly eager traders.
2. **Choose Safe Locations**:
    - Conduct trades in neutral, open areas with an agreed level of security.
    - Avoid bringing strangers into your shelter or revealing your full resources.
3. **Set Boundaries**:
    - Decide in advance how much you are willing to trade and stick to it.
    - Politely but firmly refuse trades that feel unfair or unsafe.
4. **Bring Backup**:
    - Have a trusted person accompany you for protection and support during trades.

Building Long-Term Trade Relationships

1. **Establish Trust**:
    - Honor agreements and deliver on promises to build a good reputation.
    - Avoid exploiting others' desperation, as this can damage relationships and community cohesion.
2. **Create Specialization**:
    - Focus on producing or mastering one high-demand good or skill to become indispensable in your trade network.
3. **Barter Ethics**:
    - Help those in dire need with reasonable trades, ensuring survival without taking advantage of their situation.
    - Foster a culture of fairness to strengthen community bonds.

Dealing with Disputes

1. **Neutral Mediators**:
    - Use respected community members to mediate disagreements.
2. **Document Trades**:
    - Record significant trades in writing or with witnesses to prevent misunderstandings.
3. **Conflict Resolution**:
    - Focus on finding mutually agreeable solutions to maintain trust and cooperation.

The Role of Bartering in Rebuilding Society

1. **Encouraging Collaboration**:
    - Bartering fosters interdependence, encouraging communities to work together toward shared goals.
2. **Economic Foundations**:
    - Successful trade networks can evolve into more formal systems of exchange, laying the groundwork for rebuilding economies.
3. **Promoting Innovation**:
    - Scarcity often drives creativity, with people finding new ways to use and trade goods.

Final Thoughts

Bartering and trade are not just survival tactics; they are the building blocks of a new economy in a broken world. By mastering the art of negotiation, cultivating trust, and offering value through goods or skills, you can navigate this new economic landscape effectively. More than just securing resources, bartering fosters resilience, cooperation, and hope for a better future.

Community Survival: Working Together in the Aftermath

In the aftermath of a nuclear war, survival often depends on the strength and cooperation of the community. While individuals can accomplish much, pooling resources, skills, and efforts greatly increases the chances of thriving in a hostile environment. Community survival is about building trust, fostering collaboration, and creating systems that benefit all members. This chapter explores how to work together effectively, address common challenges, and build a resilient group dynamic.

The Importance of Community in Survival

1. **Shared Resources**:
    ◦ A community can combine food, water, tools, and skills, reducing individual burdens and ensuring broader access to essentials.
    ◦ Shared efforts in resource management, such as group farming or water collection, increase efficiency.
2. **Skill Diversity**:
    ◦ Each individual brings unique abilities, from medical knowledge and mechanical repair to hunting and cooking.
    ◦ Collaboration leverages these strengths to address diverse survival needs.
3. **Emotional Support**:
    ◦ A strong community provides companionship, reducing feelings of isolation and fear.
    ◦ Group problem-solving creates a sense of purpose and hope.
4. **Enhanced Security**:
    ◦ Communities can organize defenses against external threats, such as looters or hostile individuals.
    ◦ A larger group is more intimidating and capable of mutual protection.

Establishing a Functional Community

1. Leadership and Decision-Making

- **Choose Leaders**:
    ◦ Elect leaders based on experience, trustworthiness, and ability to mediate disputes.
- **Shared Governance**:
    ◦ Create a council or committee to ensure balanced decision-making.
    ◦ Use democratic methods, like voting, to resolve major decisions.

2. Defining Roles and Responsibilities

- Assign specific tasks based on individual skills, such as:
    ◦ **Medical Care**: A person with first-aid knowledge.
    ◦ **Security**: Volunteers to patrol and protect the community.
    ◦ **Food and Water Management**: Those skilled in farming, hunting, or resource testing.
    ◦ **Logistics**: Coordinators to manage inventory, communication, and schedules.
- Rotate roles periodically to prevent burnout and encourage skill-sharing.

3. Setting Rules and Expectations

- Define acceptable behaviors and consequences for rule-breaking.
- Create agreements on resource sharing, conflict resolution, and contributions to community work.

Building Trust and Cooperation

1. **Transparent Communication**:
   - Hold regular meetings to share updates, discuss challenges, and plan actions.
   - Encourage open dialogue to ensure all voices are heard.
2. **Trust Through Action**:
   - Follow through on commitments to build credibility within the group.
   - Address disputes fairly and promptly to maintain harmony.
3. **Fostering Unity**:
   - Celebrate milestones, such as successful harvests or repairs, to boost morale.
   - Encourage collaborative projects, like building a shelter or purifying water, to strengthen bonds.

Resource Sharing and Management

1. **Creating a Centralized Inventory**:
   - Keep a detailed list of all available resources, including food, tools, and medical supplies.
   - Monitor usage to prevent shortages and ensure equitable distribution.
2. **Pooling Efforts for Resource Gathering**:
   - Assign groups to forage, hunt, or scavenge for essential supplies.
   - Share the results equally among members.
3. **Developing Sustainable Practices**:
   - Focus on renewable resources, like growing food or collecting rainwater.
   - Implement systems for waste management and resource conservation.

Addressing Common Challenges

1. Conflicts and Disputes

- **Prevention**:
  - Set clear expectations and rules to reduce misunderstandings.
- **Resolution**:
  - Use mediation or community votes to settle disputes fairly.
  - Focus on solutions that benefit the group rather than individuals.

2. Uneven Contributions

- Establish a baseline expectation for work, with exceptions for children, the elderly, or those unable to contribute physically.
- Encourage skill-sharing and mentorship to improve everyone's ability to contribute.

3. External Threats

- Organize rotating security teams to patrol and protect the community.
- Build physical defenses, such as barriers or lookout points, to deter intruders.

Fostering Long-Term Resilience

1. **Skill Development**:
   - Offer training sessions for essential skills, such as first aid, farming, or tool repair.
   - Encourage cross-training to ensure redundancy in critical tasks.
2. **Building Infrastructure**:
   - Construct shelters, water systems, and farming facilities to meet the community's needs.
   - Plan for expansion as the community grows or conditions improve.
3. **Encouraging Innovation**:
   - Support creative problem-solving and experimentation with new methods for survival.
   - Share ideas openly to improve efficiency and resource use.

Psychological and Emotional Support

1. **Creating Safe Spaces**:
   - Allow members to express concerns or fears without judgment.
   - Designate times for group relaxation or storytelling to reduce stress.
2. **Maintaining Hope**:
   - Focus on achievable goals and celebrate small successes.
   - Keep discussions about the future optimistic and solutions-oriented.
3. **Strengthening Social Bonds**:
   - Foster friendships and encourage group activities, such as shared meals or games.
   - Acknowledge the contributions of each member to reinforce their value to the community.

Building Alliances with Other Groups

1. **Exchanging Resources and Skills**:
   - Trade surplus items or expertise with nearby communities to improve overall survival.
   - Establish fair and mutually beneficial terms for exchanges.
2. **Collaborating on Projects**:
   - Work together on larger tasks, such as rebuilding infrastructure or clearing contaminated areas.
3. **Conflict Avoidance**:
   - Develop clear boundaries and agreements with neighboring groups to reduce competition or hostility.
   - Use neutral mediators if disputes arise.

Final Thoughts

Community survival requires cooperation, trust, and shared purpose. By pooling resources, assigning roles, and fostering strong relationships, a group can overcome challenges that would be insurmountable alone. In the aftermath of disaster, the strength of the community becomes the foundation for rebuilding lives, creating stability, and finding hope for a better future. Together, survival is not just possible—it becomes sustainable.

Clean Energy in the New World: Finding Safe Power Sources

In the aftermath of a nuclear war, traditional power sources like fossil fuels and centralized electricity grids will likely be unavailable or unsafe due to contamination, infrastructure damage, or long-term supply chain disruptions. Clean, renewable energy becomes the cornerstone of survival and recovery, offering sustainable power for essential tasks like lighting, heating, cooking, and communication. This chapter explores strategies for identifying and harnessing safe power sources in a post-nuclear world.

Why Clean Energy is Essential

1. **Safety**:
   - Renewable energy systems avoid reliance on potentially contaminated fuels.
   - They reduce exposure to harmful chemicals or pollutants.
2. **Sustainability**:
   - Renewable energy sources, like sunlight and wind, regenerate, providing long-term reliability.
3. **Independence**:
   - Off-grid systems empower individuals and communities to generate their own power, reducing dependency on external resources.

Clean Energy Options in a Post-Nuclear World

1. Solar Power

- **Advantages**:
   - Solar energy is abundant, renewable, and effective even in partially cloudy conditions.
- **Tools and Systems**:
   - Use photovoltaic (PV) panels to convert sunlight into electricity.
   - Pair panels with deep-cycle batteries for energy storage to use during nighttime or low-light conditions.
- **Applications**:
   - Powering small appliances, communication devices, water pumps, and lights.

2. Wind Power

- **Advantages**:
   - Wind turbines can generate electricity day and night, depending on wind availability.
- **Setup**:
   - Use salvaged materials like PVC pipes and car alternators to build small-scale wind turbines.
   - Install turbines in open, elevated locations for maximum efficiency.
- **Applications**:
   - Suitable for powering larger systems or supplementing solar energy.

3. Hydropower

- **Advantages**:
    - Continuous and consistent energy source in areas with flowing water.
- **Setup**:
    - Build small-scale water wheels or turbines to harness the kinetic energy of streams or rivers.
    - Use pipes to direct water flow for controlled energy generation.
- **Applications**:
    - Powering tools, pumps, or communal energy systems for small settlements.

4. Biomass Energy

- **Advantages**:
    - Converts organic waste, crop residues, or animal manure into energy.
- **Tools**:
    - Build biomass stoves for cooking and heating.
    - Use anaerobic digesters to produce biogas (methane) for fuel.
- **Applications**:
    - Heating shelters, cooking food, and generating biofuel for small generators.

5. Human-Powered Energy

- **Advantages**:
    - Requires no external resources and is highly reliable.
- **Examples**:
    - Hand-crank generators or pedal-powered systems for charging small devices.
    - Flywheel systems for short bursts of power.
- **Applications**:
    - Charging radios, flashlights, or phones in emergencies.

Building and Maintaining Clean Energy Systems

1. Scavenging and Salvaging

- Collect PV panels, car batteries, alternators, and other components from abandoned buildings or vehicles.
- Salvage wiring, connectors, and other materials for DIY energy projects.

2. DIY Solutions

- Build solar cookers using reflective materials like aluminum foil and cardboard.
- Construct simple wind turbines using scrap metal and repurposed motors.
- Create biomass digesters with barrels and tubing for methane production.

3. Energy Storage

- Use deep-cycle batteries or other rechargeable systems to store energy.
- Pair storage with charge controllers to prevent overloading and extend battery life.

4. System Maintenance

- Clean solar panels regularly to maintain efficiency.
- Inspect wind turbines and hydropower systems for wear and repair as needed.
- Monitor battery health and replace damaged cells promptly.

Prioritizing Energy Use

1. **Essential Needs:**
   - Focus energy on critical tasks like water purification, cooking, and powering medical devices.
   - Use energy-efficient appliances to maximize output.
2. **Lighting:**
   - Switch to LED lights, which consume less power and last longer.
   - Use solar lanterns or hand-crank flashlights as backups.
3. **Heating:**
   - Rely on passive solar heating, biomass stoves, or insulated shelters for warmth.
   - Use heat sparingly, focusing on common areas rather than heating entire spaces.
4. **Communication:**
   - Allocate energy for radios, phones, or other devices critical for staying informed or reaching help.

Combining Energy Sources for Resilience

1. **Hybrid Systems:**
   - Combine solar and wind power to cover both sunny and windy conditions.
   - Use hydropower as a continuous source and supplement with solar or biomass during high-demand periods.
2. **Redundancy:**
   - Set up multiple energy systems to ensure power availability if one source fails.
3. **Community Collaboration:**
   - Share resources and expertise to build larger, more efficient energy systems for communal use.

Challenges and Solutions

1. Limited Resources

- **Challenge:**
   - Finding and assembling components for energy systems may be difficult in resource-scarce environments.
- **Solution:**
   - Focus on scavenging and repurposing materials. Work with others to pool tools and supplies.

2. Weather Dependence

- **Challenge**:
    - Solar and wind systems are dependent on weather conditions.
- **Solution**:
    - Store excess energy during favorable conditions for later use.
    - Diversify energy sources to mitigate reliance on a single system.

3. Lack of Skills

- **Challenge**:
    - Not everyone may have the technical knowledge to build or maintain energy systems.
- **Solution**:
    - Share knowledge within your community and offer training sessions.
    - Use simple designs for DIY systems that require minimal expertise.

Long-Term Planning for Clean Energy

1. **Expand Capacity**:
    - As resources become available, upgrade or expand existing systems to increase energy output.
2. **Innovate**:
    - Experiment with new technologies, such as using geothermal heat or advanced batteries for storage.
3. **Educate Future Generations**:
    - Teach children and community members about clean energy systems to ensure continued use and maintenance.

Psychological and Practical Benefits of Clean Energy

1. **Independence**:
    - Producing your own energy reduces reliance on external sources, fostering confidence and self-reliance.
2. **Stability**:
    - Reliable energy sources improve quality of life, powering lights, heat, and tools essential for survival.
3. **Hope for Recovery**:
    - Renewable energy systems symbolize progress and resilience, serving as a foundation for rebuilding a better world.

Final Thoughts

Clean energy is not just a survival tool—it is a pathway to independence, resilience, and recovery. By harnessing renewable resources and creating sustainable systems, individuals and communities can thrive in a post-nuclear world. Through ingenuity, collaboration, and a commitment to innovation, clean energy becomes the cornerstone of a brighter, more sustainable future.

Scavenging Safely: Finding Supplies Without Risk

Scavenging in a post-nuclear world is a critical survival skill but comes with significant risks. Radiation, unstable structures, hostile encounters, and contaminated resources are constant threats. To scavenge safely, you need preparation, situational awareness, and a clear strategy for minimizing risks. This chapter explores techniques for finding supplies without compromising your safety or health.

The Importance of Safe Scavenging

1. **Access to Essential Supplies**:
   - Scavenging provides access to water, food, tools, medical supplies, and materials for shelter.
   - Salvaged items can sustain you until longer-term survival systems are established.
2. **Reducing Waste**:
   - Repurposing and salvaging ensures valuable resources don't go unused.
3. **Building Resilience**:
   - A successful scavenging strategy increases your ability to adapt and thrive.

Preparing for a Scavenging Trip

1. Understand the Risks

- **Radiation**: Fallout particles can contaminate buildings, items, and areas.
- **Structural Hazards**: Collapsed buildings or unstable debris pose dangers.
- **Hostile Encounters**: Other survivors or wildlife may view you as a threat or competition.
- **Injury**: Sharp debris, broken glass, and exposed nails can cause wounds.

2. Equip Yourself

- **Clothing**:
  - Wear sturdy, long-sleeved clothing, gloves, and steel-toed boots to protect against cuts and debris.
  - Use a waterproof or dustproof outer layer to prevent fallout particles from clinging to fabric.
- **Gear**:
  - Carry a Geiger counter to check radiation levels.
  - Bring a flashlight or headlamp for dark or enclosed spaces.
  - Include basic tools like a crowbar, knife, and multi-tool for prying, cutting, and repairs.
- **Backpack**:
  - Use a durable, lightweight pack to carry scavenged items securely.

3. Plan Your Route

- Identify nearby locations likely to have the supplies you need (e.g., grocery stores, abandoned homes, hospitals).
- Avoid high-risk areas such as blast zones or known hotspots of radiation and conflict.
- Plan your entry and exit routes carefully, considering potential obstacles or dangers.

Strategies for Safe Scavenging

1. Check Radiation Levels

- Use a Geiger counter to test the area before entering and during your search.
- Avoid spending time in areas where radiation readings exceed safe levels.
- Decontaminate items before handling them directly, especially food or water containers.

2. Prioritize Safety over Speed

- Move carefully, testing surfaces for stability before stepping or leaning.
- Avoid rushing; hurried movements increase the risk of accidents and missed dangers.

3. Stay Aware of Your Surroundings

- Monitor for structural hazards, such as crumbling walls or ceilings.
- Look for signs of other scavengers or wildlife, such as footprints, noise, or disturbed debris.
- Keep an ear out for unusual sounds, like creaking or movement, indicating instability or presence.

4. Focus on High-Yield Areas

- Prioritize locations likely to have the supplies you need:
    - **Food and Water**: Grocery stores, warehouses, restaurants, and abandoned homes.
    - **Medical Supplies**: Clinics, hospitals, pharmacies, or first-aid stations.
    - **Tools and Materials**: Hardware stores, garages, or industrial sites.
- Check overlooked places, such as small storage rooms or hidden compartments, for valuable items.

5. Work in Teams

- Pair up with trusted individuals to watch each other's backs.
- Assign roles, such as lookout and searcher, to improve efficiency and safety.
- Agree on a regrouping point in case of separation.

Managing Risks During Scavenging

1. Avoid Unnecessary Exposure

- Limit time in contaminated or high-risk areas.
- Focus on the most valuable items and leave quickly once you've gathered what you need.

2. Handle Contaminated Items Carefully

- Assume all surfaces and items are potentially contaminated.
- Use gloves and tools to handle objects, especially food or water containers.
- Wash and decontaminate scavenged items thoroughly before use.

3. Minimize Noise and Visibility

- Move quietly to avoid drawing attention from potential threats.
- Avoid using bright lights or loud tools unless absolutely necessary.

After the Scavenging Trip

1. Decontaminate Yourself and Your Gear

- Remove outer layers of clothing and seal them in plastic bags before entering your shelter.
- Wash exposed skin thoroughly with soap and clean water.
- Decontaminate tools and salvaged items using water, alcohol, or bleach solutions.

2. Inspect and Sort Items

- Check all scavenged goods for damage or contamination.
- Test food and water for safety; discard anything suspect or irradiated.
- Organize supplies to easily access critical items later.

3. Document and Reassess

- Note locations where supplies were found for future reference.
- Evaluate the risks and rewards of the trip to improve your next scavenging effort.

Avoiding Common Pitfalls

1. **Overloading**:
   - Carry only what you can manage without compromising mobility or safety.
   - Prioritize lightweight, high-value items like medical supplies or tools.
2. **Ignoring Warning Signs**:
   - Pay attention to creaking floors, unstable debris, or unusual sounds.
   - Leave immediately if the structure appears unsafe or radiation levels spike.
3. **Underestimating Contamination**:
   - Always assume surfaces and items are contaminated unless proven otherwise.
   - Use protective measures even in seemingly clean environments.

Psychological Aspects of Scavenging

1. **Stay Calm**:
   - Maintain focus and composure, even in high-pressure situations.
   - Plan breaks to manage stress and avoid exhaustion.
2. **Set Achievable Goals**:
   - Aim for specific items rather than indiscriminately searching.
   - A successful trip, no matter how small, boosts morale and confidence.
3. **Work Together**:
   - Scavenging with others reduces anxiety and provides emotional support.

- ◦ Celebrate successes as a team to strengthen bonds.

Long-Term Scavenging Strategies

1. **Track Resources**:
    - ◦ Keep a map marking scavenged locations to avoid revisiting depleted sites.
    - ◦ Identify areas likely to have untouched supplies for future trips.
2. **Replenish and Repurpose**:
    - ◦ Use scavenged items to repair or improve existing tools, clothing, and shelter.
    - ◦ Find creative ways to extend the life of limited resources.
3. **Build Community Networks**:
    - ◦ Share information about safe locations or valuable finds with trusted allies.
    - ◦ Trade scavenged items to access resources you lack.

Final Thoughts

Scavenging safely is a balance of preparation, caution, and adaptability. By understanding the risks, equipping yourself properly, and staying alert, you can gather essential supplies without endangering yourself. Scavenging is not just about survival—it's about building a foundation for recovery and resilience in a challenging world. With careful planning and execution, you can turn abandoned resources into tools for a brighter future.

Preparing for the Unpredictable: Adapting to Changing Conditions

Adapting to changing conditions in a post-nuclear world is essential for survival. The unpredictable nature of such an environment—ranging from shifting radiation levels to weather extremes, resource scarcity, and social instability—requires flexibility, preparedness, and resilience. This chapter explores strategies for adapting to these challenges while maintaining safety and stability.

Understanding the Nature of Change

1. **Environmental Shifts**:
   - Radiation levels may fluctuate due to weather patterns, such as wind or rain spreading fallout particles.
   - Long-term changes like nuclear winter or the breakdown of ecosystems can alter survival priorities.
2. **Resource Availability**:
   - Supplies of clean water, food, and medical resources may diminish or become inaccessible over time.
   - Scavenged materials may degrade or fail, requiring alternative solutions.
3. **Social Dynamics**:
   - Interactions with other survivors can range from cooperative to hostile.
   - Group structures and relationships may evolve under stress.
4. **Personal Health**:
   - Physical and mental health conditions may worsen without proper care or resources.
   - Injuries or illnesses can limit mobility and productivity.

Building a Resilient Mindset

1. **Flexibility**:
   - Be willing to change plans and strategies as new information or challenges arise.
   - Treat obstacles as opportunities to learn and improve.
2. **Proactive Thinking**:
   - Anticipate potential problems and prepare solutions in advance.
   - Focus on prevention rather than reaction to minimize risks.
3. **Emotional Resilience**:
   - Practice stress management techniques, such as mindfulness or deep breathing.
   - Stay optimistic by celebrating small victories and focusing on progress.

Adapting Survival Strategies

1. Resource Management

- **Conservation**:
  - Use resources sparingly and avoid waste.
  - Repurpose items whenever possible to extend their usefulness.
- **Stockpiling**:
  - Build reserves of essential items, such as food, water, and medical supplies.
  - Rotate stored goods to ensure they remain usable over time.

- **Alternatives**:
  - Identify substitutes for scarce resources, like purifying water with charcoal if filters run out.

2. Shelter Adjustments

- Reinforce existing shelters to withstand new threats, such as weather extremes or structural decay.
- Relocate to safer areas if current shelter becomes unsuitable due to contamination or instability.
- Adapt indoor spaces for farming or renewable energy use if outdoor conditions worsen.

3. Energy Solutions

- Diversify energy sources by combining solar, wind, and biomass systems to ensure continuity.
- Create low-energy solutions, such as passive heating or cooking techniques, to conserve power.

Navigating Environmental Changes

1. Radiation Levels

- Monitor radiation frequently using Geiger counters or dosimeters to detect changes.
- Adjust travel routes, living areas, or activities to avoid newly contaminated zones.
- Use barriers, such as additional soil or concrete, to shield against increased radiation.

2. Weather Extremes

- Prepare shelters for temperature drops during nuclear winter by improving insulation and heating.
- Collect rainwater for drinking but purify it to remove potential radioactive particles.
- Protect crops and outdoor resources with tarps, greenhouses, or other coverings.

3. Food and Water Scarcity

- Develop sustainable practices, such as indoor gardening or raising small livestock, to ensure ongoing food production.
- Use filtration, boiling, or distillation to purify water from unreliable sources.
- Explore foraging opportunities while testing for contamination to avoid exposure to unsafe food.

Managing Social Instability

1. Building Trust:

- Foster strong relationships within your community to encourage collaboration and mutual support.
- Share resources and skills selectively to build goodwill while maintaining personal safety.

2. Conflict Resolution:

- Address disputes calmly and fairly to prevent escalation.
- Use mediators or community leaders to resolve larger disagreements.

3. Safety Measures:

- Establish security protocols, such as watch rotations and designated safe zones.
- Be cautious of new individuals or groups and vet their intentions before forming alliances.

Maintaining Health and Well-Being

1. Physical Health:

- Prioritize hygiene by regularly washing and disinfecting yourself, your clothing, and your tools.
- Address injuries and illnesses promptly using first-aid supplies or natural remedies.
- Ensure proper nutrition by balancing calorie intake with vitamins and minerals from scavenged or grown food.

2. Mental Health:

- Create routines to establish a sense of normalcy and reduce anxiety.
- Engage in activities that bring joy or relaxation, such as reading, crafting, or music.
- Foster open communication within your group to share concerns and support one another.

Preparing for the Unexpected

1. **Emergency Kits:**
   - Keep a "go bag" ready with essential items like food, water, medical supplies, and communication tools.
   - Include multipurpose tools, spare batteries, and portable power sources.
2. **Skills Training:**
   - Learn new skills, such as first aid, navigation, or repair work, to handle diverse challenges.
   - Practice survival scenarios to build confidence and readiness.
3. **Backup Plans:**
   - Have alternative routes, shelters, and resource locations identified in case primary options fail.
   - Test backup systems like secondary water filters or energy sources to ensure they're functional.

Embracing Innovation and Creativity

1. **Improvisation:**
   - Use available materials creatively to solve problems or build tools.
   - Experiment with new methods for farming, energy generation, or water collection.
2. **Collaboration:**
   - Share ideas with your community to develop innovative solutions.
   - Combine resources and skills to tackle larger projects or challenges.
3. **Trial and Error:**
   - Test different approaches and refine them based on results.
   - Learn from mistakes and adapt strategies to improve outcomes.

Building Long-Term Resilience

1. **Resource Renewal**:
    - Focus on sustainable practices, such as planting crops or raising animals, to reduce dependence on finite supplies.
    - Invest in renewable energy systems for consistent power generation.
2. **Education**:
    - Teach survival skills and knowledge to others, ensuring the group's capability grows over time.
    - Record successful methods and techniques for future reference.
3. **Community Networks**:
    - Establish connections with other groups to exchange resources, knowledge, and support.
    - Build alliances for joint survival efforts and increased security.

Final Thoughts

Adapting to unpredictable conditions requires preparation, creativity, and the ability to pivot when circumstances change. By staying vigilant, flexible, and resourceful, you can not only survive but also create stability and hope in a world of uncertainty. Every challenge is an opportunity to grow stronger and more capable, ensuring that you and your community are prepared for whatever comes next.

Alternative Medicines and Remedies for Radiation Sickness

Radiation sickness, also known as acute radiation syndrome (ARS), occurs when the body is exposed to high doses of ionizing radiation. While modern medical treatments are most effective, these may be unavailable in a post-nuclear world. In such cases, alternative medicines and natural remedies can provide some relief, support the body's healing processes, and mitigate symptoms. This chapter explores alternative approaches to managing radiation sickness using available resources.

Understanding Radiation Sickness

1. **Symptoms of ARS**:
   - **Early Symptoms**: Nausea, vomiting, diarrhea, and fatigue.
   - **Intermediate Symptoms**: Skin burns, hair loss, weakened immunity, and organ damage.
   - **Late Symptoms**: Infections, anemia, and long-term cancer risks.
2. **How Radiation Affects the Body**:
   - Damages cells, particularly those that divide rapidly (e.g., blood, skin, gastrointestinal lining).
   - Causes oxidative stress, increasing free radicals that harm tissues.
3. **Goals of Alternative Treatment**:
   - Reduce oxidative damage.
   - Support immune function and cell regeneration.
   - Relieve symptoms like nausea, inflammation, and fatigue.

Natural Remedies for Radiation Sickness

1. Antioxidant-Rich Foods and Herbs

- **Why They Work**:
  - Antioxidants neutralize free radicals, reducing oxidative damage caused by radiation.
- **Examples**:
  - **Fruits**: Berries, pomegranates, and citrus fruits for vitamin C.
  - **Vegetables**: Spinach, kale, and carrots for beta-carotene.
  - **Herbs**: Turmeric (curcumin), green tea (catechins), and rosemary.
- **How to Use**:
  - Incorporate these into meals or brew as teas.

2. Adaptogenic Herbs

- **Why They Work**:
  - Help the body adapt to stress and improve overall resilience.
- **Examples**:
  - **Ashwagandha**: Boosts immune response and reduces stress.
  - **Ginseng**: Enhances energy and supports cell recovery.
  - **Holy Basil (Tulsi)**: Known for its anti-inflammatory and radioprotective properties.

- **How to Use:**
    - Prepare as teas, tinctures, or dried powder added to food.

3. Iodine and Seaweeds

- **Why They Work:**
    - Protect the thyroid from absorbing radioactive iodine (I-131).
- **Examples:**
    - Iodine-rich foods like kelp, nori, wakame, and dulse.
- **How to Use:**
    - Consume seaweed as snacks or soups; avoid overconsumption to prevent iodine toxicity.

4. Clays and Activated Charcoal

- **Why They Work:**
    - Absorb toxins and radioactive particles, reducing their impact on the body.
- **Examples:**
    - Bentonite clay and activated charcoal.
- **How to Use:**
    - Mix clay or charcoal with water and consume in small amounts.
    - Do not overuse, as these can interfere with nutrient absorption.

5. Bone Broth and Collagen

- **Why They Work:**
    - Promote gut healing, important for countering gastrointestinal damage from radiation.
- **Examples:**
    - Bone broth made from animal bones, rich in gelatin and minerals.
- **How to Use:**
    - Drink warm broth daily to soothe the digestive tract and support recovery.

6. Immune-Boosting Remedies

- **Why They Work:**
    - Strengthen the body's defense against infections.
- **Examples:**
    - Garlic: Antiviral and immune-modulating properties.
    - Echinacea: Enhances white blood cell activity.
    - Elderberry: Antioxidant-rich and supports respiratory health.
- **How to Use:**
    - Add garlic to meals, brew echinacea or elderberry as teas.

Symptom-Specific Remedies

1. Nausea and Vomiting

- **Ginger**: Brew fresh ginger tea or chew slices.
- **Peppermint**: Sip peppermint tea or use as aromatherapy.
- **Chamomile**: Calms the stomach and reduces stress.

2. Diarrhea

- **Bananas**: High in potassium, which replenishes electrolytes.
- **Rice Water**: Soothes the digestive tract and reduces dehydration.
- **Marshmallow Root**: Brew into tea for a protective mucilage layer in the gut.

3. Fatigue

- **Energy-Boosting Foods**: Nuts, seeds, honey, and dates.
- **Herbs**: Ginseng or ashwagandha to restore energy.

4. Skin Burns and Damage

- **Aloe Vera**: Apply gel to soothe burns and aid healing.
- **Calendula**: Use as a salve for inflammation and tissue repair.
- **Honey**: Antibacterial and moisturizing for damaged skin.

5. Hair Loss

- **Rosemary Oil**: Stimulates hair follicles; mix with a carrier oil and apply to the scalp.
- **Onion Juice**: Rich in sulphur, it supports hair regrowth when applied topically.

Techniques for Detoxification

1. **Hydration**:
   - Drink purified water to flush out toxins and support kidney function.
2. **Sweating**:
   - Use safe methods like light exercise or warm baths to promote detox through sweat.
   - Avoid overheating if you are already weak.
3. **Breathing Exercises**:
   - Practice deep breathing to improve oxygenation and reduce stress.

Cautions and Considerations

1. **Radiation-Specific Limitations**:
   - These remedies support symptoms and recovery but do not replace professional medical treatments like potassium iodide (KI) or chelation therapy.
2. **Allergies and Sensitivities**:
   - Test new remedies in small amounts to ensure they don't cause adverse reactions.
3. **Pregnancy and Vulnerable Groups**:
   - Pregnant women, children, and the elderly should use remedies with caution and consult knowledgeable individuals if possible.

Building a Stockpile of Remedies

1. **Herbs and Spices**:
   - Grow hardy herbs like garlic, ginger, and turmeric in small gardens or containers.
   - Store dried herbs in airtight containers for long-term use.
2. **Non-Perishable Ingredients**:
   - Stockpile items like honey, seaweed, and dried elderberries.
   - Include activated charcoal and bentonite clay in your first-aid kit.
3. **Books and Resources**:
   - Keep guides on herbal medicine and natural remedies for reference.

Final Thoughts

While alternative medicines and remedies cannot cure radiation sickness, they can alleviate symptoms, support recovery, and improve quality of life in a resource-limited environment. By understanding how to use natural ingredients and techniques effectively, you can build a holistic approach to managing radiation exposure and its effects. With careful planning and resourcefulness, these remedies can be a vital part of your survival toolkit.

Rebuilding from Rubble: Starting Over After Destruction

Rebuilding from rubble after a nuclear war is one of the most challenging and courageous endeavors survivors can undertake. The world will likely be unrecognizable, with shattered infrastructure, contaminated environments, and a devastated economy. Yet, within the chaos lies an opportunity to create something new—an adaptive, sustainable, and resilient way of life. This chapter explores strategies and principles for starting over after destruction.

Assessing the Damage

1. **Survey Your Environment**:
   - Identify the extent of destruction to buildings, roads, and other infrastructure.
   - Assess the presence of radiation or other environmental hazards using tools like Geiger counters.
2. **Evaluate Resources**:
   - Take stock of salvageable materials, tools, and supplies within the rubble.
   - Determine which natural resources, such as clean water or arable land, are accessible.
3. **Prioritize Safety**:
   - Clear immediate hazards, such as unstable debris, fires, or exposed electrical wiring.
   - Set up temporary shelters in safe zones away from contamination.

Clearing and Salvaging

1. **Clearing Rubble**:
   - Use tools like shovels, crowbars, and wheelbarrows to remove debris systematically.
   - Create designated areas for waste, salvageable materials, and hazardous items.
2. **Salvaging Materials**:
   - **Wood and Metal**: Reuse for constructing shelters or crafting tools.
   - **Bricks and Concrete**: Repurpose for rebuilding walls or fortifying structures.
   - **Glass and Plastic**: Use for windows, greenhouses, or water storage.
3. **Dealing with Contaminated Debris**:
   - Wear protective gear, including gloves and masks, when handling potentially radioactive materials.
   - Isolate contaminated items to prevent further exposure or spread.

Establishing Shelter

1. **Temporary Shelter**:
   - Use tarps, tents, or salvaged materials to create makeshift housing.
   - Prioritize insulation and weatherproofing to ensure comfort and safety.
2. **Permanent Structures**:
   - Rebuild homes and communal spaces using salvaged and natural materials.
   - Opt for simple, sturdy designs like earthbag or cob structures for durability and ease of construction.
3. **Community Hubs**:
   - Dedicate a central space for meetings, resource distribution, and shared activities.
   - Build communal kitchens, water collection systems, and storage facilities.

Restoring Basic Utilities

1. **Water Systems**:
   - Repair or build new water collection and filtration systems using salvaged pipes, barrels, or natural resources.
   - Establish communal wells or rainwater harvesting setups to ensure access to clean water.
2. **Power Generation**:
   - Use renewable energy sources like solar panels, wind turbines, or biomass generators.
   - Share energy resources among the community for lighting, cooking, and communication.
3. **Waste Management**:
   - Design composting systems for organic waste.
   - Create latrines or septic systems to manage human waste hygienically.

Reviving Food Production

1. **Gardening and Farming**:
   - Clear and test soil for contamination before planting crops.
   - Use raised beds or hydroponic systems for safer food production in contaminated areas.
2. **Livestock and Foraging**:
   - Raise hardy animals like chickens, rabbits, or goats for meat, eggs, and milk.
   - Identify and harvest safe wild plants, fruits, and fungi.
3. **Food Preservation**:
   - Build solar dehydrators or use traditional methods like salting and smoking to store food.

Rebuilding Community

1. **Leadership and Organization**:
   - Choose leaders or councils to coordinate rebuilding efforts and decision-making.
   - Establish clear roles and responsibilities based on skills and resources.
2. **Education and Training**:
   - Teach essential survival skills, such as farming, toolmaking, and first aid.
   - Share knowledge about radiation safety, sustainable living, and construction techniques.
3. **Conflict Resolution**:
   - Create systems for resolving disputes to maintain harmony and cooperation.
   - Focus on fairness and collective benefit to foster trust and unity.

Fostering Resilience

1. **Mental Health and Morale**:
   - Hold regular gatherings to share experiences, celebrate achievements, and maintain hope.
   - Provide support for those struggling with grief or trauma.
2. **Innovation and Creativity**:
   - Encourage problem-solving and experimentation with new tools, methods, or designs.
   - Use available resources in unconventional ways to meet challenges.

1. **Building for the Future**:
   - Focus on creating systems and structures that can withstand future challenges, such as extreme weather or resource scarcity.
   - Plan for long-term sustainability by incorporating renewable energy and regenerative agriculture.

Long-Term Planning

1. **Re-establishing Trade**:
   - Connect with nearby communities to exchange goods, skills, and knowledge.
   - Develop fair systems for barter and resource sharing.
2. **Education and Record-Keeping**:
   - Document rebuilding efforts, lessons learned, and new techniques for future generations.
   - Re-establish basic education for children to ensure the transfer of knowledge and skills.
3. **Adapting to New Normals**:
   - Recognize that life after destruction will be different but can still be fulfilling.
   - Focus on rebuilding not just infrastructure but also culture, community, and purpose.

Final Thoughts

Rebuilding from rubble is a monumental task, but it is also an opportunity to create a better, more resilient world. By working together, repurposing resources, and embracing adaptability, survivors can lay the foundation for a thriving community. In the face of destruction, the human spirit's capacity to rebuild and recover shines brightest, transforming adversity into a chance for renewal.

Community Survival: Working Together in the Aftermath

After a nuclear war, survival becomes a collective effort. The challenges of a post-nuclear world—scarce resources, environmental hazards, and social instability—are far too great for individuals to face alone. A well-organized, cooperative community increases the chances of survival and fosters a sense of purpose and hope. This chapter focuses on strategies for building, managing, and thriving within a community in the aftermath of destruction.

The Power of Community

1. **Shared Resources**:
    - By pooling food, water, tools, and other essentials, communities can maximize efficiency and reduce waste.
    - Group efforts in activities like farming or scavenging yield better results than individual endeavors.
2. **Diverse Skills**:
    - Each member brings unique strengths, such as medical knowledge, mechanical skills, or farming expertise.
    - Collaboration ensures that critical tasks are covered and knowledge is shared.
3. **Emotional Support**:
    - Isolation breeds despair, but a supportive community fosters resilience and mental well-being.
    - Group solidarity helps manage stress, fear, and grief.
4. **Safety in Numbers**:
    - Larger groups are better equipped to defend against external threats, such as looters or wild animals.
    - Organized security measures can protect communal resources and territory.

Building the Foundation of a Community

1. Finding and Organizing Survivors

- **Gathering Members**:
    - Seek out nearby survivors and establish contact through visible signals, notes, or radio communication.
- **Screening for Compatibility**:
    - Vet new members for skills, temperament, and trustworthiness.
    - Be cautious but inclusive to ensure a diverse and capable group.

2. Establishing Leadership

- **Choosing Leaders**:
    - Elect leaders who demonstrate fairness, competence, and decision-making skills.
- **Shared Decision-Making**:
    - Create a council or committee for collective leadership to prevent power imbalances.
- **Defined Roles**:
    - Assign responsibilities based on skills and interests, such as security, medical care, or resource management.

3. Setting Rules and Expectations

- Draft a basic code of conduct to guide behavior and resolve conflicts.
- Establish systems for resource distribution, work schedules, and decision-making processes.

Managing Resources as a Community

1. Pooling and Inventorying

- Collect and document all resources available within the group.
- Create a centralized inventory for food, water, tools, and medical supplies.

2. Sustainable Use

- Implement rationing systems for high-demand items like food and water.
- Encourage creative use of resources to minimize waste and maximize utility.

3. Sharing and Trading

- Promote fair sharing within the group to avoid resentment and inequality.
- Trade surplus items with neighboring communities to acquire needed goods.

Communication and Collaboration

1. Regular Meetings

- Hold daily or weekly meetings to discuss goals, challenges, and updates.
- Allow every member to voice concerns or contribute ideas.

2. Skill Sharing

- Organize training sessions for essential skills like first aid, farming, and tool repair.
- Encourage mentorship programs to ensure knowledge transfer within the group.

3. Conflict Resolution

- Address disputes promptly using mediators or group votes.
- Focus on solutions that prioritize fairness and group cohesion.

Building Infrastructure Together

1. Shelter

- Work as a team to construct or reinforce shelters using salvaged materials.
- Design communal areas for cooking, storage, and meetings.

2. Food and Water Systems

- Create group gardens or farms to ensure a steady food supply.
- Build water collection and purification systems for shared use.

3. Energy Solutions

- Pool resources to set up renewable energy systems, such as solar panels or wind turbines.
- Distribute power equitably for lighting, cooking, and essential tools.

Maintaining Security

1. Defensive Measures

- Establish perimeter defenses using barriers, traps, or lookout posts.
- Organize rotating patrols or watch schedules to ensure constant vigilance.

2. Emergency Plans

- Develop protocols for responding to threats, such as intruders or natural disasters.
- Practice drills to ensure everyone knows their role in emergencies.

3. Conflict Avoidance with Outsiders

- Approach unfamiliar groups cautiously and negotiate from a position of strength.
- Use barter or alliances to build positive relationships with neighboring communities.

Psychological and Emotional Well-Being

1. Community Activities

- Hold communal meals, storytelling sessions, or games to foster a sense of normalcy and unity.
- Celebrate milestones, such as successful harvests or construction projects, to boost morale.

2. Supporting Mental Health

- Encourage open dialogue about fears and challenges.
- Provide safe spaces for individuals to process grief or trauma.

3. Building Hope

- Focus on shared goals and the vision of a better future.
- Highlight achievements to remind everyone of their collective strength and progress.

Expanding the Community

1. Welcoming New Members

- Develop a process for integrating new survivors, including orientation and role assignment.
- Balance growth with resource availability to avoid overstraining the group.

2. Networking with Other Groups

- Build relationships with neighboring communities for mutual aid and trade.
- Collaborate on larger projects, such as rebuilding infrastructure or clearing contaminated areas.

3. Preparing for Long-Term Stability

- Establish systems for education, governance, and economic development.
- Invest in sustainable practices to ensure the community thrives for generations.

Final Thoughts

Surviving and thriving in the aftermath of destruction depends on the strength of the community. By working together, sharing resources, and supporting one another, survivors can overcome even the greatest challenges. A well-organized and unified group transforms despair into hope, turning ruins into a foundation for a better, more resilient future.

Navigating the Ruins: Travel Safety in the Post-Nuclear World

Traveling through a post-nuclear landscape is fraught with dangers, from radiation hotspots and structural hazards to hostile encounters and environmental challenges. Whether moving between shelters, scavenging for supplies, or searching for other survivors, safe navigation requires careful planning, situational awareness, and resourcefulness. This chapter provides essential strategies and practical advice for traveling safely in a post-nuclear world.

Understanding the Risks of Travel

1. **Radiation Exposure:**
     - Fallout may have contaminated the air, soil, and water, posing invisible dangers.
     - Certain areas, like blast zones or fallout paths, remain hazardous for extended periods.
2. **Structural Dangers:**
     - Collapsed buildings, unstable debris, and damaged infrastructure can cause injury or entrapment.
3. **Hostile Threats:**
     - Desperate individuals, armed groups, or predatory wildlife may see travelers as targets.
4. **Environmental Challenges:**
     - Extreme weather conditions, poor visibility, and contaminated water sources complicate travel.

Planning Your Journey

1. Define Your Purpose

- Identify clear objectives for the journey, such as scavenging for supplies, relocating, or contacting others.
- Evaluate if the trip is necessary or if alternatives (e.g., bartering locally) are safer.

2. Map Your Route

- Use pre-war maps to chart paths avoiding known blast zones, fallout areas, or unstable regions.
- Include detours for emergencies and identify potential safe havens along the way.

3. Check Conditions

- Monitor radiation levels using a Geiger counter to determine which areas are safe to traverse.
- Observe weather patterns and delay travel during storms or extreme conditions.

Packing Essentials for Safe Travel

1. Protective Gear

- **Clothing:** Wear long sleeves, durable pants, gloves, and boots to protect against debris and contamination.
- **Masks and Goggles:** Use N95 masks or improvised alternatives to avoid inhaling radioactive particles; goggles protect eyes from dust or debris.
- **Outer Layers:** Choose waterproof or dustproof outerwear to prevent fallout from clinging to clothing.

2. Navigation Tools

- **Compass and Maps**: Essential for navigation when landmarks are unrecognizable.
- **GPS Devices**: Useful if satellite systems remain operational, but carry backups in case of failure.
- **Markers**: Use chalk or ribbons to mark safe routes and help retrace your steps.

3. Survival Supplies

- **Water**: Carry purified water and portable filtration systems.
- **Food**: Pack lightweight, high-energy options like dried fruits, nuts, and ration bars.
- **First Aid Kit**: Include bandages, antiseptics, and any personal medications.
- **Tools**: Bring a multi-tool, knife, and flashlight with extra batteries.

Staying Safe on the Move

1. Radiation Safety

- **Monitor Levels**: Regularly check radiation levels with a Geiger counter, especially when entering new areas.
- **Avoid High-Risk Zones**: Steer clear of blast craters, downwind fallout zones, and water bodies near contamination sites.
- **Decontaminate**: Clean exposed skin and gear after traveling through potentially contaminated areas.

2. Structural Awareness

- Test floors and staircases in damaged buildings for stability before stepping.
- Avoid leaning on walls or entering areas with visible cracks, sagging, or loose debris.

3. Minimizing Hostile Encounters

- Travel quietly and avoid drawing attention with loud noises or bright lights.
- Stick to concealed paths or natural cover, like forests or hillsides, to reduce visibility.
- Keep a safe distance from other travelers until their intentions are clear.

4. Traveling with a Group

- Appoint a leader or navigator to manage direction and decisions.
- Assign roles, such as lookout or scout, to distribute responsibilities.
- Stay close enough for mutual support but maintain spacing to minimize risks from potential ambushes.

Overcoming Environmental Challenges

1. Weather

- Carry gear for extreme conditions, such as thermal blankets for cold or tarps for rain.
- Seek shelter during severe weather, avoiding exposed or unstable areas.

2. Water Sources

- Test water for radiation and contaminants before drinking.
- Avoid stagnant water or sources near industrial ruins, which are more likely to be polluted.

3. Land Navigation

- Use natural landmarks, like rivers or ridgelines, when artificial markers are unreliable.
- Be cautious of natural traps, such as sinkholes or concealed pits.

Emergency Responses

1. **Injury**:
   - Treat minor wounds immediately to prevent infection; use antiseptics and bandages.
   - For major injuries, prioritize stabilization and seek a safe place to rest and recover.
2. **Getting Lost**:
   - Retrace your steps using marked trails or familiar landmarks.
   - Signal for help using reflective surfaces, loud whistles, or signal fires.
3. **Encountering Hostility**:
   - Avoid confrontation by retreating or hiding if possible.
   - If forced to engage, use defensive tools like pepper spray or improvised weapons.

Long-Term Travel Strategies

1. Establish Safe Routes

- Mark and document reliable paths to key locations, such as water sources or trade hubs.
- Share route maps with trusted individuals to create a network of safe passage.

2. Relay Points

- Set up small caches of supplies along frequently used routes to reduce travel burdens.
- Use abandoned buildings or natural shelters as waystations.

3. Develop Partnerships

- Coordinate with nearby groups to share information about safe zones, dangers, and resources.
- Create agreements for mutual aid during travel, such as escort services or shared supplies.

Psychological Considerations

1. **Stay Focused**:
   - Keep your objective in mind to avoid unnecessary risks or distractions.
2. **Manage Fear**:
   - Recognize that fear is natural but focus on actionable steps to stay in control.

1. **Work Together**:
   - Support traveling companions through encouragement and shared responsibilities.

Final Thoughts

Traveling in a post-nuclear world demands preparation, vigilance, and adaptability. By understanding the risks, equipping yourself properly, and practicing safe navigation techniques, you can minimize dangers and achieve your objectives. Every journey is a step toward survival, recovery, and the rebuilding of a better future. Safe travels are not just about reaching a destination—they are about ensuring you have the means to thrive when you get there.

Bartering and Trade: The New Economy in a Broken World

In the aftermath of a nuclear war, the collapse of traditional economies will force survivors to create a new system for exchanging goods, skills, and services. Bartering and trade will become the foundation of this post-apocalyptic economy, enabling individuals and communities to access essential resources and build cooperative networks. This chapter explores the principles of bartering, how to trade safely, and what items and skills are likely to hold the most value in a broken world.

The Importance of Bartering and Trade

1. **Access to Essential Resources**:
   - No single person or group can possess everything they need to survive.
   - Bartering allows survivors to exchange surplus goods or specialized skills for critical supplies.
2. **Encouraging Cooperation**:
   - Trade fosters relationships and alliances between individuals and communities.
   - Collaborative exchanges strengthen bonds and increase mutual survival chances.
3. **Resource Efficiency**:
   - Bartering prevents waste by giving unused or surplus items a purpose.
   - It encourages creative problem-solving and innovation with limited resources.

High-Value Items for Bartering

1. Essentials

- **Food**: Long-lasting items like canned goods, rice, beans, and dried fruits.
- **Water**: Clean water or water purification tools like filters and tablets.
- **Medical Supplies**: Bandages, antibiotics, antiseptics, and over-the-counter medications.

2. Energy and Fuel

- **Batteries**: Especially rechargeable ones.
- **Fuel**: Gasoline, propane, or firewood.
- **Solar Chargers**: For powering small devices like radios or flashlights.

3. Tools and Equipment

- **Multi-Tools**: Compact and versatile.
- **Repair Kits**: For clothing, tools, or vehicles.
- **Weapons and Ammunition**: For hunting or protection (use with caution in trade).

4. Hygiene and Personal Care

- Soap, toothpaste, menstrual products, and disinfectants like bleach.
- Baby supplies such as diapers or formula.

5. Comfort and Luxury Items

- Tobacco, alcohol, coffee, and chocolate for morale and enjoyment.
- Books, playing cards, or small toys for psychological relief.

High-Value Skills for Bartering

1. **Medical Knowledge**:
     - Providing first aid, treating wounds, or diagnosing illnesses.
2. **Repair and Maintenance**:
     - Fixing tools, vehicles, or electronics.
3. **Food Production**:
     - Farming, hunting, fishing, or preserving food.
4. **Security and Defense**:
     - Protecting individuals or communities, training others in self-defense.
5. **Teaching and Knowledge**:
     - Sharing skills like building, cooking, or crafting.

Establishing a Bartering System

1. Assess What You Have

- Identify surplus items or skills you can offer in trade.
- Organize these resources for easy access during negotiations.

2. Understand Needs and Value

- Determine what items or services are in high demand within your area.
- Research the perceived value of goods to avoid over- or under-trading.

3. Set Up Fair Exchanges

- Use mutually agreed benchmarks to assess the value of goods or services (e.g., a certain amount of food for a specific tool).
- Ensure both parties feel satisfied with the trade to build trust and foster future cooperation.

Safe Trading Practices

1. Choose Neutral Locations

- Conduct trades in open, neutral areas where both parties feel safe.
- Avoid revealing your shelter or resource stockpiles to prevent future targeting.

2. Bring Backup

- If possible, trade with a trusted companion who can provide support or security.
- Agree on signals or plans in case of danger.

3. Inspect Goods before Trading

- Check the quality and usability of traded items.
- Test consumables, such as food or water, for contamination.

4. Be Prepared for Negotiation

- Enter trades with a clear understanding of your bottom line.
- Stay respectful but firm, and walk away if the deal feels unfair or unsafe.

Building Trade Networks

1. Local Networks

- Establish regular trading relationships with nearby survivors or groups.
- Create a sense of community through shared exchanges and mutual trust.

2. Regional Trade Hubs

- Organize or participate in larger trade gatherings where multiple groups can barter.
- Set rules for fairness and security to ensure smooth exchanges.

3. Specialization

- Focus on producing or mastering one high-demand good or skill to increase your trade value.
- Partner with others who complement your strengths to expand your offerings.

Managing Bartering Challenges

1. Conflict and Disputes

- Address disagreements calmly and openly to preserve trust.
- Use mediators or impartial third parties to resolve serious disputes.

2. Scammers and Thieves

- Be wary of trades that seem too good to be true.
- Verify the reputation of trading partners through references or observation.

3. Fluctuating Value

- Understand that the value of goods can change based on supply, demand, and season.
- Adapt your trading strategy to meet current market conditions.

Long-Term Bartering Strategies

1. Stockpiling and Preparation

- Build reserves of high-value items like medical supplies, seeds, and tools.
- Preserve surplus food or water for future trades.

2. Education and Skill-Building

- Learn new skills to expand your tradeable services.
- Train others in your community to increase collective resources.

3. Strengthening Alliances

- Form alliances with other groups to secure safe trade routes and shared resources.
- Collaborate on large-scale projects, such as farming or infrastructure rebuilding.

Psychological and Social Benefits of Trade

1. **Fostering Relationships**:
    - Trade creates opportunities to interact and build trust with others.
    - Collaborative exchanges strengthen community bonds.
2. **Encouraging Innovation**:
    - The need for bartering drives creative solutions to resource shortages.
    - New tools or methods often emerge from shared knowledge.
3. **Restoring Hope**:
    - Successful trades provide tangible proof of progress and recovery.
    - A thriving trade network symbolizes stability in a chaotic world.

Final Thoughts

Bartering and trade are more than survival mechanisms—they are the seeds of rebuilding a functioning society. By understanding the value of goods and skills, practicing safe trading methods, and fostering cooperation, survivors can create a new economy that supports recovery and growth. In the ashes of destruction, trade represents a step toward stability, resilience, and a better future.

Fire Safety in Fallout Zones: Managing Risks in Destruction

In a post-nuclear world, the risk of fire is ever-present. Fallout zones are filled with flammable debris, unstable structures, and hazardous materials, creating a dangerous environment where fires can easily ignite and spread. Moreover, radioactive particles can complicate firefighting efforts, making fire safety an essential survival skill. This chapter explores how to prevent, manage, and respond to fires in fallout zones to protect yourself, your community, and your resources.

The Unique Risks of Fire in Fallout Zones

1. **Flammable Debris**:
   - Widespread destruction leaves large amounts of dry wood, paper, plastics, and other highly flammable materials.
   - Broken gas lines or exposed fuel sources increase the risk of sudden ignition.
2. **Hazardous Materials**:
   - Industrial ruins and damaged infrastructure may contain chemicals or radioactive substances that worsen fires or release toxic fumes.
3. **Compromised Water Supply**:
   - Access to clean water may be limited, making firefighting more challenging.
4. **Radiation Complications**:
   - Fallout particles can spread further during fires, contaminating air and surrounding areas.
   - Smoke from radioactive materials poses additional health risks.

Preventing Fires in Fallout Zones

1. Clearing and Organizing Debris

- **Create Firebreaks**:
  - Remove flammable materials from around shelters or key resource areas.
  - Clear vegetation, debris, and loose paper to minimize fire spread.
- **Separate Hazards**:
  - Store fuel, gas canisters, and flammable chemicals away from living areas and each other.
- **Dispose of Waste Safely**:
  - Burn trash only in controlled environments with proper ventilation and at a safe distance.

2. Safe Use of Fire

- **Cooking and Heating**:
  - Use stoves or fire pits designed to contain flames and sparks.
  - Avoid open flames indoors unless proper ventilation is available.
- **Lighting**:
  - Opt for battery-powered lanterns or solar lights instead of candles or oil lamps.
- **Smoking**:
  - Designate safe smoking areas far from flammable debris.

3. Electrical Safety

- **Inspect Wiring:**
    - Check salvaged electrical devices and wiring for damage before use.
- **Avoid Overloading Circuits:**
    - Use low-power devices and avoid makeshift electrical setups that could overheat.

Preparing for Fire Emergencies

1. Firefighting Supplies

- Stockpile tools like fire extinguishers, buckets, and shovels.
- Keep large quantities of sand or soil to smother flames in case water is unavailable.
- Build makeshift fire blankets using heavy fabrics soaked in water.

2. Early Warning Systems

- Assign lookouts to monitor for smoke or flames, especially during dry or windy conditions.
- Use whistles or bells to alert others quickly in case of fire.

3. Evacuation Plans

- Map out multiple escape routes from shelters or community areas.
- Practice fire drills to ensure everyone knows how to respond.

4. Fire Safety Zones

- Designate safe zones free of flammable materials where people can retreat during fires.
- Build shelters with non-combustible materials, such as metal or stone.

Managing Fires in Fallout Zones

1. Smothering Small Fires

- Use sand, soil, or fire blankets to extinguish flames without spreading fallout particles.
- Avoid using water on fires involving electrical equipment or chemical fuels.

2. Containing Larger Fires

- Dig trenches around the fire to create a firebreak and prevent its spread.
- Remove nearby flammable materials to reduce fuel for the fire.
- If water is available, direct it at the base of the flames to extinguish them effectively.

3. Dealing with Chemical Fires

- Do not use water on fires caused by flammable liquids, such as oil or gasoline, as this can spread the flames.
- Use specialized extinguishers or dry powders if available, or smother with soil.

Protecting Yourself from Smoke and Radiation

1. Respiratory Protection

- Wear N95 masks or improvised respirators to filter out smoke and radioactive particles.
- Wet a cloth and cover your mouth and nose if proper masks are unavailable.

2. Skin Protection

- Cover exposed skin with thick clothing to prevent burns and contamination from radioactive fallout.
- Avoid direct contact with smoke or ash from fires in fallout zones.

3. Avoiding Toxic Fumes

- Stay upwind of the fire to minimize exposure to hazardous smoke.
- Evacuate the area quickly if industrial chemicals or radioactive materials are involved.

Post-Fire Clean-up and Safety

1. Checking for Hotspots

- After extinguishing a fire, check the area for smoldering debris that could reignite.
- Use water, sand, or soil to cool any remaining embers.

2. Decontaminating the Area

- Clear ash and debris while wearing protective gear to avoid exposure to fallout particles.
- Dispose of contaminated materials in sealed containers away from living areas.

3. Assessing Damage

- Inspect shelters and resources for structural damage or contamination.
- Repair or replace critical infrastructure promptly.

Community Fire Safety Strategies

1. **Shared Resources:**
   - Pool firefighting tools and supplies for communal use.
   - Build and maintain shared water reserves or firebreaks around community areas.
2. **Collaborative Training:**
   - Teach fire prevention and firefighting skills to all community members.
   - Practice coordinated responses to fires during community drills.
3. **Mutual Support:**
   - Work together to extinguish fires, evacuate vulnerable individuals, and rebuild affected areas.
   - Share lessons learned from fire incidents to improve future preparedness.

Psychological Aspects of Fire Safety

1. **Staying Calm:**
   - Panic can worsen fire situations. Focus on following your emergency plan and using available resources effectively.
2. **Supporting Each Other:**
   - Encourage cooperation and maintain morale by emphasizing community strength and resilience.
3. **Learning from Fires:**
   - Use each fire incident as an opportunity to refine your prevention and response strategies.

Final Thoughts

Fire safety in fallout zones is an ongoing challenge, but with preparation, vigilance, and teamwork, it can be managed effectively. By understanding the unique risks posed by this environment and adopting proactive measures, survivors can protect themselves, their resources, and their communities. Fire, when controlled, is a tool for survival; when unchecked, it is a devastating force. In a world of destruction, mastering fire safety becomes a vital step toward rebuilding and resilience.

Protecting the Next Generation: Teaching Children Survival Skills

In the aftermath of a nuclear war, ensuring the survival and well-being of children is paramount. They represent hope and the future of any rebuilding efforts. Teaching children practical survival skills not only increases their chances of staying safe but also empowers them to contribute to their community and adapt to the challenges of a post-nuclear world. This chapter explores effective strategies for teaching children essential survival skills in an age-appropriate and engaging manner.

Why Teaching Survival Skills Matters

1. **Building Independence**:
   - Equipping children with knowledge and skills allows them to handle emergencies and basic tasks confidently.
2. **Reducing Fear**:
   - Understanding what to do in dangerous situations can alleviate anxiety and foster a sense of security.
3. **Preparing Future Leaders**:
   - Children who learn survival skills early are better prepared to take on responsibilities and contribute to the community.
4. **Ensuring Continuity**:
   - Passing on survival knowledge helps preserve critical skills and traditions for future generations.

Principles of Teaching Survival Skills

1. **Age Appropriateness**:
   - Tailor lessons to a child's age, maturity, and physical abilities.
   - Use simple, hands-on methods for younger children and more detailed explanations for older ones.
2. **Safety First**:
   - Ensure all training activities are conducted in a safe, controlled environment.
   - Emphasize the importance of caution and thinking before acting.
3. **Repetition and Practice**:
   - Reinforce lessons through repetition and practical exercises to build confidence and muscle memory.
4. **Encouragement and Support**:
   - Celebrate successes to build self-esteem and motivation.
   - Provide gentle guidance and patience when children struggle with new skills.

Essential Survival Skills for Children

1. Basic First Aid

- Teach children how to:
  - Clean and bandage minor wounds.
  - Recognize symptoms of dehydration, heatstroke, or hypothermia.
  - Administer basic treatments, like applying pressure to stop bleeding.
- Use simple, memorable steps, such as the acronym "STOP" for wound care: Stop bleeding, Treat, Observe, Protect.

2. Finding and Purifying Water

- Explain the importance of clean water for health and survival.
- Show them how to:
    - Identify safe water sources, like rainwater or filtered streams.
    - Use simple purification methods, such as boiling or filtering through cloth.
- Practice water collection techniques using improvised tools like tarps or containers.

3. Identifying Safe Foods

- Teach children to:
    - Recognize edible plants, berries, and insects common in your area.
    - Avoid potentially poisonous foods using easy-to-remember rules, like the "5 Senses Test" (smell, touch, taste, etc., in small steps).
- Incorporate foraging walks into lessons for hands-on experience.

4. Building and Maintaining Shelter

- Show children how to:
    - Collect and arrange materials like branches, leaves, or tarps to build a basic shelter.
    - Identify safe locations, such as elevated areas away from flooding or unstable debris.
- Practice constructing small shelters together as a family activity.

5. Fire Safety and Use

- Teach fire safety rules, such as:
    - Always have water or soil ready to extinguish flames.
    - Never leave a fire unattended.
- Introduce older children to fire-starting techniques using flint, matches, or magnifying glasses in a safe setting.

6. Navigation and Orientation

- Explain how to:
    - Use the sun, stars, or landmarks for direction.
    - Read maps and understand basic compass use.
- Practice navigating familiar areas before moving to more challenging terrain.

7. Emergency Communication

- Teach children to:
    - Recognize and use signals like whistles, hand gestures, or flashlight codes.
    - Memorize important phrases or locations to communicate needs or seek help.
- Role-play scenarios to reinforce these lessons.

Teaching Strategies for Different Age Groups

1. Younger Children (Ages 4–7)

- Focus on simple, repetitive tasks, such as washing hands or recognizing danger symbols.
- Use stories, songs, or games to make learning fun and engaging.
- Emphasize "do's" (e.g., "Stay near shelter") over "don'ts."

2. Older Children (Ages 8–12)

- Introduce more complex skills, like knot tying, basic tool use, or identifying edible plants.
- Allow hands-on practice under supervision to build confidence.
- Incorporate teamwork exercises, such as group shelter-building.

3. Teenagers (Ages 13+)

- Teach advanced skills, like foraging, fishing, or basic mechanical repairs.
- Encourage leadership roles in group activities to foster responsibility.
- Discuss problem-solving and critical thinking in survival scenarios.

Creating a Survival Skills Curriculum

1. **Daily Tasks:**
   - Integrate survival skills into daily routines, like collecting water or cooking.
   - Assign small, manageable responsibilities to children.
2. **Themed Lessons:**
   - Dedicate specific days to focus on particular skills, such as "Water Wednesday" or "Fire Safety Friday."
3. **Skill Challenges:**
   - Organize friendly competitions to test knowledge, like building the fastest shelter or purifying the most water.
4. **Story-Based Learning:**
   - Use fictional or historical survival stories to illustrate concepts and spark interest.

Reinforcing Mental and Emotional Resilience

1. **Managing Fear:**
   - Teach children calming techniques, such as deep breathing or focusing on positive outcomes.
   - Reassure them that it's okay to feel scared and encourage open discussions about their fears.
2. **Encouraging Problem-Solving:**
   - Pose "what if" scenarios to stimulate critical thinking and adaptability.
   - Reward creative solutions and reinforce the idea that mistakes are part of learning.
3. **Fostering Teamwork:**
   - Emphasize the importance of cooperation and mutual support.
   - Highlight how their contributions benefit the entire group.

Involving Children in Community Efforts

1. **Group Activities**:
   - Organize survival skill workshops or games for children within the community.
   - Encourage peer teaching, where older children mentor younger ones.
2. **Shared Responsibilities**:
   - Assign age-appropriate community tasks, such as tending gardens or assisting with repairs.
   - Recognize and celebrate their efforts to build pride and a sense of purpose.
3. **Creating a Safe Environment**:
   - Foster a community culture of support and respect for children's contributions.
   - Provide safe spaces where children can play, learn, and grow despite the challenges.

Final Thoughts

Teaching children survival skills is about more than preparing them for emergencies—it's about empowering them to thrive in adversity. By equipping the next generation with practical knowledge, emotional resilience, and a sense of purpose, you ensure that they not only survive but contribute meaningfully to rebuilding a better future. With patience, creativity, and encouragement, you can help children navigate the challenges of a post-nuclear world with confidence and hope.

Preserving Knowledge: Libraries and Education in Survival

In a world rebuilt from the ruins of nuclear destruction, knowledge is one of the most powerful tools for survival and recovery. The preservation of knowledge ensures that the lessons of the past and the skills needed for the future are accessible to all. Establishing makeshift libraries and fostering education can provide communities with the information necessary to navigate challenges, innovate solutions, and lay the groundwork for a better tomorrow. This chapter explores strategies for preserving knowledge and fostering education in survival settings.

The Importance of Preserving Knowledge

1. **Survival Skills**:
   - Guides on farming, medical care, construction, and toolmaking become invaluable in a world without modern conveniences.
   - Historical lessons on overcoming adversity provide inspiration and practical insights.
2. **Innovation and Progress**:
   - Science, engineering, and technology texts enable communities to rebuild infrastructure and develop new solutions.
   - Shared knowledge fosters creativity and collaboration.
3. **Cultural Continuity**:
   - Preserving literature, art, and history maintains a sense of identity and connection to the past.
   - Stories, songs, and traditions inspire hope and unity.
4. **Education for the Next Generation**:
   - Teaching children and young adults ensures that critical skills and values are passed down.
   - Education empowers the next generation to lead, innovate, and thrive.

Creating and Maintaining Libraries

1. Gathering Resources

- **Books and Manuals**:
  - Prioritize practical subjects like first aid, farming, mechanics, and survival skills.
  - Include diverse texts covering history, literature, science, and art.
- **Digital Archives**:
  - Salvage e-readers, tablets, and laptops along with solar chargers to access stored digital libraries.
- **Oral Histories**:
  - Record and share knowledge from experienced community members.

2. Protecting Materials

- **Physical Preservation**:
  - Store books in waterproof, sealed containers to prevent damage from moisture or pests.
  - Use shelving systems in dry, secure locations to reduce wear and tear.
- **Digital Backups**:
  - Maintain multiple copies of critical information on USB drives or memory cards.

○ Power devices with renewable energy sources like solar chargers to ensure accessibility.

3. Organizing Information

- Create a simple catalog system, grouping materials by subject or purpose.
- Use color coding or symbols for non-readers to identify categories like health, food, or construction.

4. Expanding the Collection

- Encourage community members to contribute books, manuals, and knowledge.
- Scavenge libraries, schools, and abandoned homes for additional resources.
- Share and exchange materials with neighboring communities.

Education in Survival Settings

1. Establishing Schools

- **Location**:
  - ○ Use a communal space, such as a large tent, abandoned building, or outdoor area, for classes.
- **Instructors**:
  - ○ Identify community members with teaching experience or specialized knowledge.
- **Curriculum**:
  - ○ Focus on practical skills like reading, math, and critical thinking alongside survival subjects.

2. Teaching Methods

- **Hands-On Learning**:
  - ○ Emphasize experiential activities, such as gardening, toolmaking, or first aid drills.
- **Storytelling**:
  - ○ Use engaging narratives to teach history, ethics, and problem-solving.
- **Peer Teaching**:
  - ○ Encourage older children and adults to mentor younger learners, fostering a culture of shared knowledge.

3. Balancing Education with Survival

- Incorporate education into daily activities, such as teaching math during food rationing or science while purifying water.
- Allow flexibility for children and adults to contribute to essential tasks without sacrificing learning opportunities.

Knowledge for Community Development

1. Practical Skills Training

- Teach essential skills like farming, carpentry, first aid, and navigation.
- Offer workshops on renewable energy, waste management, and resource conservation.

2. Health and Hygiene Education

- Share knowledge about disease prevention, sanitation, and nutrition.
- Provide basic medical training for treating injuries and illnesses.

3. Community Governance

- Teach conflict resolution, leadership, and organizational skills.
- Foster an understanding of cooperation, fairness, and decision-making processes.

Passing Knowledge to the Next Generation

1. **Apprenticeships**:
    - Pair young learners with skilled community members for hands-on training in trades like blacksmithing, farming, or medicine.
2. **Cultural Preservation**:
    - Encourage storytelling, music, and art to keep cultural heritage alive.
    - Document and teach traditional recipes, crafts, and ceremonies.
3. **Developing New Leaders**:
    - Teach critical thinking, ethics, and adaptability to prepare future leaders.
    - Provide opportunities for young adults to take on responsibilities and make decisions.

Collaborative Knowledge Sharing

1. **Community Networks**:
    - Establish relationships with neighboring groups to exchange resources and expertise.
    - Organize regional gatherings for shared education and trade.
2. **Traveling Teachers and Libraries**:
    - Create mobile libraries or teaching teams to bring knowledge to isolated communities.
    - Use portable storage solutions for books and materials to ensure accessibility.
3. **Oral Knowledge Banks**:
    - Record and disseminate oral histories, survival techniques, and community lessons.

Challenges and Solutions

1. **Limited Resources**:
   - Focus on collecting and preserving high-priority texts and skills.
   - Use creative methods like memorization or simple diagrams to convey complex ideas.
2. **Access and Security**:
   - Protect libraries from theft or environmental damage with secure, well-hidden storage.
   - Rotate access to digital devices to conserve power and prevent overuse.
3. **Maintaining Interest**:
   - Make learning engaging through interactive activities, storytelling, and games.
   - Emphasize the importance of knowledge as a tool for survival and growth.

Psychological Benefits of Education and Libraries

1. **Fostering Hope**:
   - Learning offers a sense of purpose and progress in difficult times.
   - Libraries and schools symbolize stability and the possibility of a better future.
2. **Building Community**:
   - Shared educational experiences strengthen bonds and create a collective identity.
   - Knowledge exchange encourages collaboration and mutual support.
3. **Encouraging Creativity**:
   - Exposure to literature, art, and science inspires innovation and problem-solving.

Final Thoughts

Preserving knowledge and fostering education are critical to rebuilding a world after devastation. Libraries and schools serve as beacons of hope and hubs of progress, equipping survivors with the tools they need to overcome challenges and create a brighter future. By prioritizing the preservation and sharing of knowledge, you ensure that the lessons of the past and the possibilities of the future remain within reach.

Post-War Government: Navigating New Power Structures

After a nuclear war, traditional government systems are likely to collapse, leaving a vacuum of authority and order. In this void, new power structures often emerge, ranging from small community councils to regional alliances or authoritarian regimes. Understanding how to navigate and contribute to these evolving systems is critical for survival and long-term stability. This chapter explores the formation of post-war governance, the challenges and opportunities it presents, and strategies for establishing fair and functional power structures.

The Collapse of Traditional Governance

1. **Loss of Central Authority**:
   - Communication breakdowns, destruction of infrastructure, and loss of leadership disrupt established governments.
   - Regional and local authorities may become isolated, forcing communities to fend for themselves.
2. **Rise of New Power Centers**:
   - Local leaders, military groups, or organized survivors often step into the power vacuum.
   - Competing factions may vie for control, leading to instability or conflict.
3. **Survivor Dependency**:
   - In the absence of organized systems, communities depend on mutual aid, resource pooling, and local decision-making.

Types of Post-War Power Structures

1. Community-Based Governance

- **Characteristics**:
  - Small, localized groups prioritize collective survival and resource management.
  - Decisions are often made democratically or through consensus.
- **Strengths**:
  - Adaptable to local needs and conditions.
  - Encourages collaboration and fairness.
- **Challenges**:
  - Limited resources and influence; vulnerable to external threats.

2. Militarized Leadership

- **Characteristics**:
  - Former military personnel or armed groups take control, prioritizing security and order.
- **Strengths**:
  - Effective in enforcing rules and defending against threats.
- **Challenges**:
  - Risk of authoritarianism; potential for conflict with civilian populations.

3. Authoritarian Regimes

- **Characteristics**:
    - Single leaders or small groups assert control, often using fear or force.
- **Strengths**:
    - Quick decision-making and strong enforcement.
- **Challenges**:
    - Potential for abuse of power and oppression.

4. Federated Alliances

- **Characteristics**:
    - Neighboring communities form coalitions to share resources and address common challenges.
- **Strengths**:
    - Pooling of resources and expertise; greater influence in negotiations.
- **Challenges**:
    - Coordination difficulties; risk of internal disputes.

Forming a Fair and Functional Government

1. Defining Leadership

- **Selecting Leaders**:
    - Choose individuals based on competence, trustworthiness, and community respect.
    - Rotate leadership roles or establish term limits to prevent power consolidation.
- **Sharing Power**:
    - Use councils or committees to distribute decision-making authority.

2. Creating Rules and Systems

- **Code of Conduct**:
    - Establish clear guidelines for behavior, resource use, and conflict resolution.
- **Enforcement**:
    - Develop fair systems for addressing rule violations, such as mediation or communal votes.
- **Adaptability**:
    - Allow for amendments to rules as conditions and needs evolve.

3. Building Trust and Transparency

- **Open Communication**:
    - Hold regular meetings to share updates, discuss challenges, and gather feedback.
- **Accountability**:
    - Require leaders to report their actions and decisions to the community.

Navigating Challenges in Post-War Governance

1. Resource Management

- **Equitable Distribution**:
    - Allocate food, water, and supplies based on need and contribution.
- **Sustainability**:
    - Focus on renewable resources and efficient systems to ensure long-term survival.

2. Security and Defense

- **Internal Security**:
    - Establish protocols to address disputes, theft, or rule violations within the community.
- **External Threats**:
    - Organize defenses against hostile groups or environmental hazards.

3. Conflict Resolution

- **Mediation**:
    - Use neutral parties to resolve disputes fairly and peacefully.
- **Community Involvement**:
    - Encourage collective problem-solving to foster unity.

Collaborating with Other Groups

1. Establishing Alliances

- Build relationships with neighboring communities to share resources, knowledge, and security.
- Negotiate agreements on trade, defense, and mutual aid.

2. Managing Conflicts

- Use diplomacy to resolve disputes with other groups before they escalate.
- Avoid resource hoarding or aggressive expansion that could provoke conflict.

3. Developing Regional Systems

- Work toward creating regional councils or federations for coordinated decision-making.
- Share leadership roles and responsibilities to balance power.

The Role of Education and Knowledge

1. **Preserving Governance Knowledge**:
    - Salvage books and documents on government systems, law, and ethics.
    - Use these resources to guide the creation of fair and functional systems.

1. **Teaching Leadership Skills**:
    - Train future leaders in negotiation, organization, and decision-making.
    - Emphasize the importance of fairness, transparency, and community well-being.
2. **Encouraging Civic Participation**:
    - Involve all community members in governance to ensure diverse perspectives and shared responsibility.
    - Use education to foster understanding of rights, responsibilities, and the value of cooperation.

Maintaining Stability in New Power Structures

1. **Preventing Corruption**:
    - Establish checks and balances to hold leaders accountable.
    - Rotate roles and responsibilities to prevent power hoarding.
2. **Adapting to Change**:
    - Reassess governance systems regularly to address new challenges and opportunities.
    - Encourage innovation and experimentation with solutions.
3. **Promoting Unity**:
    - Focus on shared goals and values to reduce divisions.
    - Celebrate community achievements to strengthen morale and cohesion.

Final Thoughts

Navigating and contributing to new power structures after a nuclear war requires adaptability, collaboration, and a commitment to fairness. Whether through small community councils or larger regional alliances, effective governance is critical for survival and rebuilding. By fostering trust, preserving knowledge, and prioritizing collective well-being, survivors can create systems that not only sustain life but also pave the way for a more equitable and resilient society.

I hope you found important information here within the covers of this book. If you liked this book, please leave a review where you bought it. Thank you from the author.